Maintaining Earth's Oceans

ENVIRONMENT AT RISK

Maintaining Earth's Oceans

ANN HEINRICHS

Marshall Cavendish
Benchmark
New York

Other Marshall Cavendish Offices:
Marshall Cavendish International (Asia) Private Limited, 1 New Industrial Road, Singapore 536196 • Marshall Cavendish International (Thailand) Co Ltd. 253 Asoke, 12th Flr, Sukhumvit 21 Road, Klongtoey Nua, Wattana, Bangkok 10110, Thailand • Marshall Cavendish (Malaysia) Sdn Bhd, Times Subang, Lot 46, Subang Hi-Tech Industrial Park, Batu Tiga, 40000 Shah Alam, Selangor Darul Ehsan, Malaysia

Marshall Cavendish is a trademark of Times Publishing Limited

All websites were available and accurate when this book was sent to press.

Library of Congress Cataloging-in-Publication Data

Heinrichs, Ann.
Maintaining earth's oceans / Ann Heinrichs.
p. cm. — (Environment at risk)
Includes bibliographical references and index.
Summary: "Provides comprehensive information on Earth's oceans, their importance, and the environmental threats placed upon them"— Provided by publisher.
ISBN 978-1-60870-479-8 (print) ISBN 978-1-60870-677-8 (ebook)
1. Ocean—Environmental aspects. 2. Marine ecology. 3. Marine pollution. 4. Environmental degradation.
I. Title.
GC26.H45 2012
333.91'64—dc22
2010025188

Editor: Christine Florie
Publisher: Michelle Bisson
Art Director: Anahid Hamparian
Series Designer: Sonia Chaghatzbanian

Expert Reader: Nathalie Reyns, Ph.D., assistant professor, Marine Science and Environmental Studies, University of San Diego, San Diego, California

Photo research by Marybeth Kavanagh

Cover photo by *Pacific Stock/SuperStock*

The photographs in this book are used by permission and through the courtesy of: *Getty Images*: Yva Momatiuk & John Eastcott/Minden Pictures, 2-3, 5, 33; Chris Newbert/Minden Pictures, 26; Chris Wilkins/ AFP, 49; Popperfoto, 64; *Cutcaster*: Brandon Seidel, back cover, 2, 14, 32, 46, 48, 60, 75; *Super Stock*: IndexStock, 6, 57, 68; All Canada Photos, 20; Robert Harding Picture Library, 22, 62; Hemis.fr, 28; Science Faction, 41, 52; age fotostock, 55; *The Image Works*: Michael Good/Impact/HIP, 9; RIA Novosti/TopFoto, 40; Avampini/V&W, 70; Jeff Greenberg, 82; *AP Images*: Press Association, 10; Charlie Riedel, 44; Louiz Rocha, Papahānaumokuākea Marine National Monument, 80; *Alamy*: Ace Stock Limited, 13; The Natural History Museum, 17; David Olsen, 24; Leslie Garland Picture Library, 30; Rosanne Tackaberry, 34, Alaska Stock LLC, 59; Jack Hill, 66; Stephen Dorey, 74; *Photo Researchers, Inc.*: Gary Hincks, 15; US Geological Survey, 18; SPL, 19; *Newscom*: KRT, 76; *Envision*: Curzon Studio, 84

Printed in Malaysia (T)
1 3 5 6 4 2

Contents

One
Freedom of the Sea

"[T]he sea is common to all, because it is so limitless that it cannot become a possession of any one, and because it is adapted for the use of all. . . ." So wrote the Dutch scholar Hugo Grotius in his 1609 book *The Freedom of the Sea*. A vision of the limitless ocean still persists in our mind's eye. That vision is based in reality: we live on only a small portion of our planet. Oceans cover about 71 percent of Earth's surface and hold 97 percent of Earth's water.

No matter where we live, our lives are profoundly dependent on the sea. Oceans shape our climate, provide us with food, connect us with other nations, and give us avenues of exploration and trade. They support almost half of all species on Earth, supplying 20 percent of the animal protein that humans consume. From the depths of the ocean come powerful energy resources and life-saving medicines.

Earth's oceans cover almost three-fourths of our planet's surface. Maintaining and protecting them ensures their health for generations to come.

The economic value of the oceans is tremendous. For millennia, people of coastal lands have depended on the sea for their livelihood. Today fisheries are a major sector of the economy in industrialized nations such as Japan and even more vital in underdeveloped coastal nations. The U.S. economy, too, depends on ocean-related industries. Economists estimate that one out of every six jobs in the United States is related to the oceans through fishing, boating, shipping, recreation, tourism, and other coastal industries. Furthermore, the coastal zone is the basis for one-third of the nation's gross domestic product.

As bountiful as the oceans are, their bounty is not as limitless as a gaze across the sea would suggest. World population almost quadrupled in the twentieth century, from 1.6 billion in 1900 to 6.1 billion in 2000. This growth vastly expanded the world's economic activities, with drastic consequences for the oceans. Many fish populations have dwindled through overfishing, with some species being fished to extinction. Wastes poison the waters, and seafoods introduce toxins into the human diet. Oil spills not only pollute vast expanses of ocean water and miles of shorelines but also kill off marine species and coastal wildlife. Gases acidify the ocean water, endangering countless species. Industrial and vehicle emissions surround the earth with excess carbon dioxide, which causes temperatures in both the air and the water to rise.

Grotius's "freedom of the sea" concept reigned in the world's consciousness for centuries. By the mid–twentieth century, this idea gave way to the realization that the oceans need to be managed. In response to environmental threats, the international community began regulating the use of ocean waters. UN agencies drew up international agreements to control fisheries, curb ocean pollution, preserve biodiversity, and protect marine habitats. As a result of these agreements, we have internationally recognized fishing-rights boundaries and pollution-control standards. Individual nations have followed suit with their own legislation. At the same time, scientific research has expanded our global outlook on the oceans.

Protecting Earth's oceans is an international issue. Here, a pollution control boat patrols Victoria Harbor in Hong Kong, China.

A nation's control over the sea was once believed to extend about 3 nautical miles (3.45 miles) from shore. That three-mile limit sprang partly from the seventeenth-century "cannon-shot rule"—that a nation had jurisdiction over its waters as far as it could fire a cannon from the shore in defense. Now, however, the focus has changed from defense to responsibility as we realize how events in one part of the ocean impact the world community. Ship debris from the Pacific Ocean shows up in Scotland. Plastic bags litter the shores of Antarctica, hundreds of miles from the nearest town. Industrial wastes in Asia enter the bodies of fish that end up on a dinner table in Kansas. No longer is any region isolated, with its impact on the ocean limited to a few miles offshore. In a 2008 study of the world's oceans, environmental scientists found that all ocean areas, however remote from human settlement, were influenced by human activity in some way, and 41 percent of the regions studied were strongly affected by human factors.

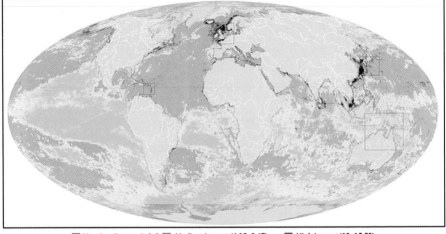

Very Low Impact (<1.4) ☐ Medium Impact (4.95–8.47)   High Impact (12–15.52)
Low Impact (1.4–4.95) ☐ Medium High Impact (8.47–12) ■ Very High Impact (>15.52)

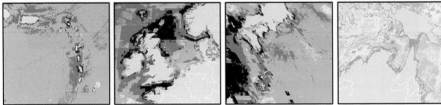

Eastern Caribbean   North Sea   Japanese Waters   Torres Straight

This global map, issued in 2008, shows the overall impact that human activities are having on marine ecosystems.

New challenges arise in the twenty-first century as we face climate change, species loss, and ocean acidification. We must work harder than ever to restore, maintain, and protect the oceans' resources. As the concept of ocean management evolves, it becomes apparent that it is not enough to hand down laws and punish those who break them. Ocean management, both international and local, calls for an enlightened approach to ocean-based activities not only on the part of governments but also on the part of industries, trade groups, and individual citizens in their everyday lives. All must consider the environmental impact of their actions, whether scientific, economic, social, or recreational. All must answer a hard question: How can we flourish today without destroying the future?

"Freedom of the sea" once meant freedom to pursue bound-less ventures in the oceans. That idea worked when fewer than a billion people walked the earth and only a fraction of them exploited the sea. Now a global community of more than 6 billion people shares the ocean as a common resource. Now is the time to move forward from exploitation to stewardship of that resource. Only then will future generations enjoy the bounty of the sea.

- The term *marine* relates to salty ocean waters, as opposed to the term *aquatic*, which refers to waters in general.

- Technically, a sea is a smaller branch of an ocean. In common usage, however, *ocean* and *sea* are used interchangeably.

Two

Ocean Features and Properties

Ocean waters are really one continuous body of water, sometimes called the World Ocean. Reaching out above the surface are islands of land, some tiny and some the large landmasses we call continents. Traditionally we divide the World Ocean into several ocean areas according to their locations and common features. Over time, people have counted anywhere from three to seven oceans. Today the five generally accepted oceans are the Atlantic, Pacific, Indian, Arctic, and Southern (or Antarctic) oceans.

The largest ocean is the Pacific Ocean, an immense expanse of water extending from the continents of Asia and Australia on the west to North and South America on the east. Next in size is the Atlantic Ocean, between North and South America on the west and Europe and Africa on the east. The Atlantic is less than half the size of the Pacific Ocean. The Indian Ocean lies between Africa and Australia, reaching northward to southern Asia and southward to Antarctica. The Southern Ocean encircles the continent of Antarctica, which lies atop the South Pole. Smallest of all is the Arctic Ocean, covering the region around the North Pole. Most of its water is frozen as a thick, drifting pack of ice.

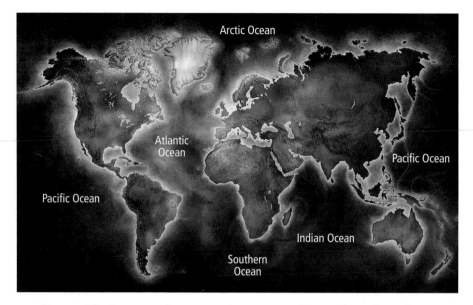

The world's five generally accepted oceans are the Arctic, Pacific, Indian, Southern, and Atlantic oceans.

The Hydrologic Cycle

Oceans play a critical role in the climate and overall well-being of the planet. They are the basis of the hydrologic cycle, the process by which water continuously recirculates between Earth and the atmosphere. This process takes place in three basic steps. First, water evaporates from the oceans and other open bodies of water, releasing water vapor into the atmosphere. Next, the water vapor condenses to form clouds. Finally, the water returns to land through precipitation in the form of rain, snow, and other falling moisture. Once on land, the water may evaporate; it may be taken up by plants, which release water vapor into the air through a process called transpiration. It may soak into the soil or flow as runoff into lakes, rivers, and streams. Runoff from land, rivers, and streams eventually reaches the oceans, where the hydrologic cycle begins again.

The Carbon Cycle and Carbon Sinks

The carbon cycle is another recirculation system. It involves the exchange of carbon between organisms (or organic material)

The Official Five

The International Hydrographic Organization (IHO) is the international agency that describes and measures oceans. The IHO once recognized four oceans—the Atlantic, Pacific, Indian, and Arctic. In 2000, it declared a fifth ocean—the Southern Ocean, surrounding Antarctica. However, some geographers still consider the Southern Ocean an extension of other, larger oceans.

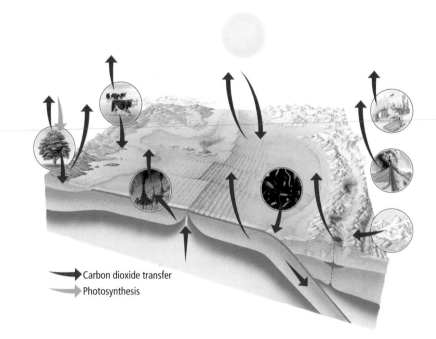

Carbon dioxide transfer
Photosynthesis

The carbon cycle, illustrated above, is the recirculation and exchange of carbon between organisms and the environment.

and the environment. On a simple level, the carbon cycle can be seen in the processes of photosynthesis and respiration. Through photosynthesis, plants absorb carbon dioxide (CO_2) from the atmosphere and release oxygen. During respiration, humans and other animals take in oxygen and exhale CO_2. Amazingly, the photosynthesis of marine plants produces at least half of all the oxygen humans breathe.

For most of human history, the carbon cycle operated in a state of equilibrium, with the absorption and release of CO_2 in balance. The cycle even accommodated fires, which consume oxygen and release CO_2. However, as human activities have poured more CO_2 into the air through vehicle emissions, industrial facilities, and power plants, the balance has gotten upset. This imbalance casts a greater focus on Earth's carbon sinks.

A carbon sink is a natural feature that absorbs or stores more carbon than it releases. The value of carbon sinks is that they can

help create equilibrium in the atmosphere by removing excess CO_2. One example of a carbon sink is a large forest. Its mass of plants and other organic material absorb and store tons of carbon. The planet's major carbon sink, however, is its oceans.

Since the Industrial Revolution began in the eighteenth century, CO_2 released during industrial processes has greatly increased the proportion of carbon in the atmosphere. Carbon sinks have been able to absorb about half of this excess CO_2, and the world's oceans have done the major part of that job. They absorb about one-fourth of humans' industrial carbon emissions, doing half the work of all Earth's carbon sinks combined.

Like kitchen sinks, the ocean sinks can fill up, though. The Southern Ocean, the strongest ocean sink, has taken in about 15 percent of the world's excess CO_2. However, a multinational scientific survey completed in 2007 has shown that this ocean is reaching its carbon saturation point. Clearly, the oceans do not have an infinite capacity to absorb carbon. As their absorption capacity weakens, the buildup of CO_2 and other so-called greenhouse gases in the atmosphere increases, the result being a worldwide warming of the climate. (The validity of the global-warming theory is widely but not universally accepted within the international scientific community.)

The Ocean Landscape

Each continent's landmass extends from the shoreline down into the water. The relatively shallow underwater region is the continental shelf, which extends to a point called the continental shelf break, where the seabed drops off sharply into the continental slope. These slopes are marked by steep-walled submarine canyons, some measuring thousands of feet deep. Beyond the continental slope is the continental rise, where currents have deposited tons of sediment in a gently sloping pile. Together, the continental shelf, slope, and rise are called the continental margin. Beyond the continental margin is the floor of the ocean basin, also called the abyssal plain.

Far from being a vast plain, the ocean floor is as diverse as the land above water. Besides plains, it features hills and

This diagram of the ocean floor shows features such as oceanic ridges and seamounts.

valleys, high mountain ridges, and deep canyons. The deepest parts of the ocean are the deep-sea trenches. Deepest of all is the Mariana Trench in the western North Pacific Ocean. It is more than 35,000 feet (10,670 meters) deep—more than six miles. If Mount Everest, Earth's highest peak, were set on the floor of the Mariana Trench, more than a mile of water would be left in the trench above it. Sea life flourishes even down in the trench. A Japanese research team explored the Mariana Trench in 1995 and found spiny, cucumber-shaped sea slugs; flat, scaly worms; and some shrimp.

Scattered across the ocean floor are thousands of mountains called seamounts, which began as volcanoes. Other mountains are part of long mountain chains, or mid–ocean ridges, that rise from the seafloor. They built up over time through volcanic activity in the underlying crust. Along each ridge's spine is a deep valley, or rift, where plates of Earth's crust diverge, or separate. As the plates shift, cracks open up, and seawater seeps through to the magma, or molten rock, simmering below. When the water heats up, it spews up through

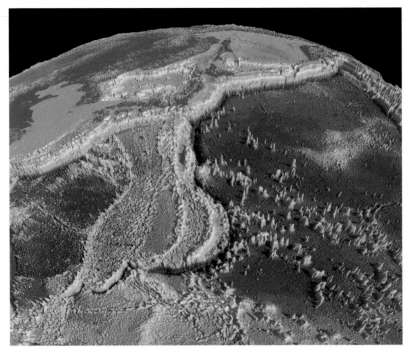

A computer model highlights the region around the Mariana Trench (purple area), Earth's deepest point.

holes in the seafloor called hydrothermal vents. These rising streams of superhot water reach temperatures as high as 750 degrees Fahrenheit (400 degrees Celsius). The vents harbor many remarkable marine organisms, as well as copper, manganese, gold, and other valuable minerals.

Ocean Movements

Ocean waters are constantly in motion even when they seem calm. Ocean currents constitute one type of motion. Flowing through the ocean like giant rivers, they move seawater around the planet. Currents are caused by factors such as winds and Earth's rotation. Two of the strongest currents are the Kuroshio Current and the Gulf Stream. The Kuroshio Current flows through the North Pacific Ocean, off the coast of Japan. The Gulf Stream moves north from the Gulf of Mexico up to the North Carolina coast. Then it drifts northeastward across the North Atlantic Ocean, where it splits off in two directions. These currents can move as fast as 4.5 miles (7.2 kilometers) an hour—more than 100 miles (161 km) a day.

Driven by global wind systems, currents swirl in large, circular loops called gyres. Gyres in the Northern Hemisphere rotate in a clockwise direction, while those in the Southern Hemisphere spin counterclockwise. Earth's five major oceanic gyres are the North Pacific, South Pacific, North Atlantic, South Atlantic, and Indian Ocean gyres. Unfortunately, gyres can pick up marine debris and trap it in the swirling current indefinitely.

Tides are another type of ocean movement. Tides are the regular rise and fall of the ocean's surface, caused mainly by the gravitational attraction of the moon. The moon, pulling on the water nearest to it, makes a bulge in the ocean. Meanwhile, waters on the opposite side of the earth resist the pull due to inertia, thus bulging at the same time. These two bulges create high tides, with water rising high up onto the seashore.

This satellite image of Earth illustrates the ocean currents that flow around the world. Warm currents are in red, cold in blue.

Waters in between the bulges are then "stretched," creating low tides, where coastal waters recede and expose more land.

The difference between a coast's water level at high tide and low tide is called its tidal range. Canada's Bay of Fundy experiences the planet's most extreme tidal range: its tides rise as high as 53 feet (16 m) twice a day.

Cycles of high and low tides occur within a period of twenty-four hours and fifty minutes, the time it takes the moon to orbit the earth—one lunar day. Most seacoasts get two high tides and two low tides every lunar day, although some places get just one high and low tide a day or two high and low tides of varying heights.

Ocean Water

Seawater is saline, or salty, because it is full of dissolved minerals called salts. The most plentiful sea salts, in order of abundance, are chlorine, sodium, sulfur (in the form of the sulfate ion SO_4^{2-}), magnesium, calcium, and potassium.

At low tide, boats at Canada's Hall's Harbour in the Bay of Fundy rest on the harbor's floor until high tide, when ocean water will fill it up.

Oceanographers calculate salinity in terms of parts of salt per 1,000 parts of water. On average, seawater has a salinity of 35. That is, it contains 35 grams of salt per liter (1,000 grams) of water and is thus 3.5 percent salt. Most of that salt is sodium chloride (NaCl)—table salt, the type you sprinkle on your food. Buoyancy—the ability of an object to float—is greater in seawater than in freshwater because the added weight of the salts increases the seawater's density.

Most of the ocean's salts wash from rocks and soil on Earth's surface. Although freshwater falls as precipitation and enters the waterways through rivers, the salt concentration at the ocean's surface becomes more dense as water evaporates. Salinity varies by location. Regions where glaciers are melting or rivers are entering the ocean are less salty than the open sea. Salinity increases in polar areas where sea ice is freezing or in tropical areas where the evaporation rate is high. Marine organisms have adapted to the level of salinity where they live. However, their survival is threatened by salts entering the oceans as sewage or runoff from fertilizers and road salts.

In terms of temperature, the ocean has three layers: the surface, the thermocline, and the deep ocean. The surface layer is the warmest because it gets heat directly from the sun. Though the average is about 62.6 °F (17 °C), surface temperatures can range from 96.8 °F (36 °C) in the Indian Ocean's Persian Gulf to 28.4 °F (−2 °C) in the polar seas. In the thermocline, the boundary between the surface and the deep layer, temperatures plunge rapidly. Below the thermocline the water is very cold; much of the deep layer has temperatures between 32 and 37.5 °F (0–3 °C). Water here does not freeze because it is so salty. Saltwater's freezing point is lower than freshwater's. Freshwater freezes at 32 °F (0 °C), but seawater with a salinity of 35 freezes at about 28.5 °F (−1.9 °C). Since most marine organisms live within a narrow temperature range, they are threatened by so-called thermal pollution when normal ocean-temperature ranges fluctuate through factors such as hot-water discharges from industrial plants.

Water pressure is another feature of the oceans. At sea level, air has a pressure of 14.7 pounds per square inch (psi; 14.7 psi

Ice from Iceland's Jokulsarlon Glacier melts into this lagoon, lowering the water's salinity level.

22

is called 1 atmosphere of pressure). Because water is heavier than air, it exerts more pressure. For every 33 feet (10 m) you descend underwater, the pressure increases by another 14.7 psi. At 99 feet (30 m) underwater, for example, the pressure is 58.8 psi, or 4 atmospheres. For humans, a pressure this high endangers air spaces in the body—the lungs, ear canals, and sinuses. Submarines and other deep-sea vessels must have heavy walls; otherwise, the water pressure would crush them. However, sperm whales and certain other marine mammals can tolerate more than 200 atmospheres with no adverse effects. Elephant seals and beaked whales are other deep divers. Scientists are studying these animals' physiology to understand how they can survive these high pressures.

Ocean Zones

Scientists use several parameters to define the major ocean zones. Marine ecologists, who study the environment of marine creatures, divide the ocean into the benthic zone (the seafloor) and the pelagic zone (open waters). The pelagic zone is further divided into the littoral, neritic, and oceanic zones.

The littoral zone, the area nearest to the shore, is subdivided into three zones. In the supralittoral zone (also called the supratidal or spray zone), water covers the shore only during very high tides or storms. The intertidal zone is the stretch of land between the high-tide and low-tide points. The sublittoral (or subtidal) zone, always covered by seawater, extends outward from the low-tide point to a depth of 660 feet (200 m). The intertidal and subtidal zones together are often called the neritic zone. Also called the coastal waters, the neritic zone comprises the waters above the continental shelf and around islands. Where the continental shelf drops off, the oceanic zone begins. All the rest of the ocean's waters lie in the oceanic zone.

Light penetration is another common parameter for defining ocean zones. Sunlight can make its way through ocean water down to about 660 feet (200 m). This upper region is called the photic, or euphotic, zone. Here live trillions of microscopic creatures called plankton. Some are animals (zooplankton),

and others are plants (phytoplankton) that use sunlight to produce nutrients, a process called photosynthesis. Phytoplankton are at the bottom of the ocean food chain and thus are the basis of all life in the oceans. About 90 percent of all sea life lives in the photic zone, including sharks, whales, jellyfish, sea turtles, and lobsters.

Below the photic zone, reaching down to about 3,280 feet (1,000 m), is the so-called twilight zone (also called the disphotic zone). Some sunlight filters down to this depth, but not enough for photosynthesis to take place. Therefore, no plants inhabit the twilight zone. Beyond the twilight zone is the midnight zone, also called the aphotic (lightless) zone. It gets no light whatsoever; the water is frigid, and the water pressure is tremendous.

A green sea turtle swims in the photic zone near Maui, Hawaii.

Ocean Habitats

The ocean itself is defined as a habitat, or type of environment, for living organisms. To describe the ocean's organisms as living in a marine habitat, however, is as uninformative as saying a land animal lives in a terrestrial habitat. Like the land, the ocean has many habitats, each with animals and plants that are specially adapted to their environment. Some of those habitats are estuaries, kelp forests, and coral reefs.

Estuaries are partly enclosed waters where freshwater and salty ocean water mix. Currents and tides routinely push in seawater, while rivers provide a constant outward flow of freshwater. Many kinds of clams, oysters, crabs, snails, and sponges, some feeding on others, live among estuaries' sea grasses and algae. Birds, mammals, snakes, and turtles from the surrounding wetlands share this habitat. Life in estuaries can be threatened by wastes and sediment that wash downstream from rivers, as well as by pollutants that roll in from the sea.

Kelp forests are underwater thickets of long-bladed algae called kelp, which grow near rocky coastlines. Many creatures spend their life in these forests. Among the benthic (seafloor) species are sea urchins, sea cucumbers, sea stars, and sponges. Farther up in the water column, fish such as giant sea bass swim through the forest eating smaller species. Scientists have done extensive research on the kelp-forest ecosystem (an ecosystem is a community of interdependent organisms). Pollution and overfishing are major factors that upset the balance of this ecosystem.

Coral reefs are complex but fragile ecosystems whose communities include fish, crabs, shrimp, and sponges. The reefs are made up of millions of corals, or tiny sea polyps. When a polyp dies, its calcium carbonate skeleton remains and becomes part of the reef. Corals come in a dazzling variety of colors and shapes. Their colors come from pigments in zooxanthellae, a type of algae that lives in coral tissues. When coral polyps become stressed, they eject the algae and turn white. Called coral bleaching, this condition can lead to the corals' death. Causes of coral bleaching include changes in temperature or salinity and excess sunlight, sediment, or CO_2.

Coral reefs are an ocean habitat that becomes "stressed" when ocean temperatures and salinity change.

Amazing though it seems, a thriving community of organisms flourishes around the scalding-hot hydrothermal vents. They include shrimp, anemones, crabs, giant tubeworms, and huge clams. Their habitat is relatively safe for now because it is too difficult to mine the valuable minerals there. Other marine habitats may be less secure. Waste disposal, mineral extraction, coastal land development, overfishing, and many other human activities put these ecosystems at risk.

Three

Waste Disposal, Runoff, and Dumping

For untold centuries, people have used the ocean as the ultimate dumping ground, a place to deposit unwanted things forever without a second thought. Pollutants and wastes of all kinds end up in the ocean, from mercury and other toxic elements to sneakers and old tires. These materials may come from sources on land, in the air, or at sea. Unfortunately, things humans put into the oceans can devastate water quality, marine ecosystems, and marine life.

Environmentalists define two types of pollution according to their point of origin. Point-source pollution comes from a specific source that can be pinpointed, such as a factory smokestack or a sewage pipe. This type of pollution is easier to measure and regulate because it originates from a known location. Nonpoint-source pollution has vague, widely scattered sources that cannot be specifically identified.

Point-Source Pollution

Ocean pollution can originate from many different kinds of industrial facilities, including power plants, paper mills, oil refineries, car factories, and food processing plants. All of them have effluent, or discharged water, with some kind of pollutants in it. The pollutants may be metals, salts, oil or grease, or bacteria or other microorganisms.

Some plants treat their own effluent on the premises by cleaning it of pollutants before discharging it. Plants in the United States may test the effluent daily, weekly, or monthly to meet water-quality standards according to the National Pollutant Discharge Elimination System (NPDES) program. Other plants send their effluent to a municipal sewage treatment facility. Some industrial plants discharge their effluent directly into local waterways, which eventually flow into an ocean.

Sewage treatment facilities treat human wastes, which include everything that "goes down the drain" in kitchens and bathrooms. U.S. sewage facilities, too, must follow stringent NPDES treatment protocols before releasing the wastewater back into the waterways.

Large farms and feedlots for cattle, pigs, and chickens are also considered bases for point-source pollution because they

The Wharf de La Salie in Landes, France, disposes paper mill and water treatment plant waste directly into the sea.

generate such large quantities of animal waste. They are called concentrated animal feeding operations (CAFOs). Many CAFOs manage their wastes responsibly, with no harmful impact on local waterways. However, some CAFOs obtain an NPDES permit but do not comply with its requirements. Others do not bother to obtain a permit at all. Under the U.S. Clean Water Act, the Environmental Protection Agency (EPA) has the job of enforcing these land-based water pollution violations.

Nonpoint-Source Pollution: Hard to Combat

Because many controls are already in place for point-source pollution, environmental scientists are increasingly studying the effects of nonpoint-source pollution—a major offender when it comes to ocean pollution. Most nonpoint-source pollution happens as a result of runoff—that is, the rain or melted snow that moves across the land or through the ground. Along the way, the water picks up all kinds of pollutants from yards, streets, homes, businesses, fields, and farms.

Runoff is hard to combat because it originates from many sources that may not be obvious. Ocean pollutants may originate far from the coast, coming from septic tanks, cars, and trucks. Rain showers drenching a ranch or farm wash fertilizers, pesticides, and animal wastes into a river and eventually to the sea. Similarly, a car on the street or in a parking lot leaks oil and grease that is washed away by rain. Loose soil from fields, construction sites, and logging areas is swept into waterways, where it clouds the water with sediments that are harmful to fish and other creatures. Pollutants that enter the rivers eventually reach the oceans.

The runoff of fertilizers from farms, lawns, and gardens is especially harmful to coastal waters. Commercial chemical fertilizers typically contain nitrogen (N) and phosphorus (P). (Phosphorus also enters the waterways as a component of sewage and many laundry detergents.) The increase in levels of N and P in the water is known as eutrophication. These chemicals are essential nutrients for algae. Where excess N and P enter the water, the algae grow and reproduce quickly. This overabundance of algae is known as an algal bloom.

Runoff and pollution have spoiled this stream in England.
Eventually, its waters will empty into the ocean.

When the algae die, they sink and decompose. The decaying process, which consumes oxygen that is dissolved in the water, creates a condition called hypoxia, or lack of oxygen. Fish, shellfish, and other marine life in the area then suffocate because they cannot draw enough oxygen from the water to survive. These so-called dead zones can be identified by large areas of algal blooms and dead fish. Scientists have identified approximately four hundred dead zones around the world, and the number of these zones is increasing. The Gulf of Mexico's dead zone is the largest in the United States.

Ocean pollution can also originate from sources at sea, such as large cargo ships. According to the UN Environment Programme, more than 90 percent of international trade takes place aboard oceangoing vessels. This seaborne trade contributes enormously to the world economy. The downside is that merchant ships can pollute the oceans with sewage, litter, garbage, dumped cargo, and oily discharges. Cruise ships for tourists can also be pollution sources. Even though international law

Table 1. Sources of Marine Pollution

Source	Percentage
Runoff and land-based discharges, such as city, farm, and industrial wastes	44%
Land-based discharges through the atmosphere, such as vehicle and industrial emissions and weapons testing	33%
Maritime transportation, such as oil ship discharges	12%
Dumping of wastes, such as sewage, Carbon dioxide (CO_2), and industrial and radioactive wastes	10%
Offshore productions, such as oil exploration and mining	1%
TOTAL	**100%**

Source: Convention on the Prevention of Marine Pollution by Dumping of Wastes and Other Matter: Background. International Maritime Organization. February 28, 2007. www.imo.org/home.asp?topic_id=1488 (accessed May 20, 2010).

regulates many of these activities, ship pollution can go unde-
tected on the open seas. Recreational boaters can pollute the
waters, too, through careless fuel spills, defective sanitary systems, or faulty marina pumping stations.

Garbage and Other Debris

Another way of polluting the ocean is by littering it with debris.
Waste disposal in the ocean may be a thoughtless activity, such
as tossing out a plastic bottle or leaving debris on a beach. It
may be an accident, as when a plastic bag is swept away in an
ocean breeze. It may be intentional; if someone's rowboat has
a gaping hole in the bottom, the easiest way to dispose of it
may be to let it sink.

Among the most shocking environmental impacts of waste
disposal are the ocean's so-called garbage patches. They are
massive accumulations of debris swept together in ocean gyres.
These phenomena occur where several currents converge and
spiral around a central point, creating a continuously swirling,
elliptical vortex. Ocean sailor Jo Royle says a gyre is like "a
giant oceanic toilet that never flushes." The largest of the ocean's
five major gyres is the North Pacific Gyre, where the Great Pacific
Garbage Patch is. A huge garbage patch has been found in the
North Atlantic Ocean, too.

Scientists estimate that about 260 million tons of plastic are
manufactured every year, and about 10 percent of that ends up
in the oceans. Seventy percent of that plastic eventually sinks
down into the water, while the rest remains floating on the
surface. Although large objects are the most visible, most of the
oceans' plastic debris is made up of tiny fragments of broken-
up plastic that are barely visible and easily consumed by small
organisms near the bottom of the food chain. Cleaning up the
debris presents problems because the garbage patches are so
large and because straining the water to capture the plastic
fragments would also trap small marine organisms.

Garbage washing up on beaches or carelessly discarded
there is hazardous to wildlife as well. The Midway Islands in
the Pacific Ocean are home to many seabird species, including
the world's largest colony of albatrosses. Theoretically, their

The Great Pacific Garbage Patch

Floating in the North Pacific Ocean is a massive collection of garbage. It's been named the Great Pacific Garbage Patch. Estimates of its extent range from the size of Texas to the size of the continental United States. Most of the garbage is plastics, including plastic bottles, plastic bags, Styrofoam, fishing lines, fishing nets, toys, and flip-flops. Rubber tires and aluminum beverage cans are in there, too. The debris gets swept up in the North

Pacific Gyre, a confluence of ocean currents, where it circulates indefinitely.

Fish, sea turtles, seabirds, and other marine wildlife get tangled up in the garbage or choke on it. Some creatures eat it and survive, enabling the garbage to return to humans in seafood. Most of the debris can barely be seen, though, as it consists of tiny plastic fragments or pellets.

habitat is protected as both a wildlife refuge and a U.S. Marine National Monument. Nevertheless, as the birds feed on fish and shellfish, they routinely consume garbage. When wildlife manager Matt Brown cut open a dead albatross, he found a toothbrush handle, a bottle cap, and some fishing net in its stomach. Some albatross chicks, he said, never fly off to forage for food because their stomachs are full of plastic. Among the coastal debris here are plastic cigarette lighters, fishing floats, bottles, plastic sheeting, toys, flashlights, and deodorant sticks. As Brown says, it takes "a global effort to solve this problem."

Ocean Dumping: An Ongoing Debate

The term *ocean dumping* has a specific meaning: disposing of waste materials by deliberately placing them into dump sites in the ocean. Old ships, sewage sludge, construction materials, and many other wastes are routinely hauled out to sea and dumped. All these materials can be harmful to marine life and human life as well.

An adult albatross and her chick are dwarfed by a pile of marine debris collected by volunteers on Midway Island.

Some types of dumping are unregulated, while others take place according to strict local, national, or international rules. For example, U.S. and international laws allow power plants and other industrial facilities to dispose of their CO_2 waste by converting it into liquid and injecting it into rock formations deep beneath the seabed. This process is known as geological sequestration (GS), part of a larger process known as carbon capture and storage (CCS). However, these facilities are not allowed to inject the CO_2 directly into the water. Disposal of radioactive wastes in the ocean was allowed until 1994, when it was banned by international law. Often it takes decades to determine the environmental impact of dumping. In the 1940s, for example, the U.S. military discarded tons of weapons in underwater dump sites off the Hawaiian coast. U.S. law prohibited weapons dumping in 1972, but studies of the environmental effects of the weapons are still going on.

Although ocean dumping of certain materials is allowed if strict standards are met, the practice will continue to be a contentious issue. Any number of accidents can happen in the course of dumping. Drums and canisters of wastes can degrade, develop cracks, or break open. Disposal vessels can collide or run aground. Just as problematic is the fact that various parties do not always agree on what constitutes safe, clean water. That issue is pertinent not only to dumping but to all aspects of ocean management.

Differing Views on Water Cleanliness

According to the International Maritime Organization (IMO), the greatest source of marine pollution is runoff and land-based discharges such as city, farm, and industrial wastes. These pollution sources can never be eliminated completely; some pollutants are naturally occurring materials that erode from the soil. However, human-generated pollutants can be minimized via regulations from the local to the international level. What degree of pollution is an "acceptable" level? There is no general, worldwide agreement on this question. To get an idea of the range of viewpoints on clean ocean water, it is interesting to examine various scientific standards set for clean drinking water.

Table 2. Safety Standards for Selected Contaminants in Drinking Water

Substance	Max. Level (mg/l)		Health Effects of Consumption	Sources of Contaminant
	EPA	WHO		
Arsenic	0.01	0.01	Skin damage; circulatory system problems; increased cancer risk	Erosion of natural deposits; runoff from orchards; runoff from glass and electronics production wastes
Cyanide	0.20	0.07	Nerve damage; thyroid problems	Discharge from steel/metal factories and plastic and fertilizer factories
Endrin	0.002	0.0006	Liver problems	Residue of insecticide (now banned in the United States)
Flouride	4.0	1.5	Bone disease; children may get mottled teeth	Water additive to strengthen teeth; erosion of natural deposits; discharge from fertilizer and aluminum factories

Sources: "Drinking Water Contaminants." U.S. Environmental Protection Agency. www.epa.gov/safewater/contaminants/index.html; *Guidelines for Drinking-Water Quality*, 3rd ed, Annex 4: Chemical summary tables. Geneva: World Health Organization, 2008, pp. 491–493. www.who.int/entity/water_sanitation_health/dwq/GDWAN4rev1and2.pdf (accessed August 5, 2010).

Substance	Max. Level (mg/l)		Health Effects of Consumption	Sources of Contaminant
	EPA	WHO		
Mercury	0.002	0.006	Kidney damage	Erosion of natural deposits; discharge from refineries and factories; runoff from landfills and farms
Nitrate	10.0	50.0	Serious illness for infants under six months	Runoff from fertilizers; leaching from septic tanks, sewage; erosion of natural deposits
2,4-D	0.07	0.03	Kidney, liver, or adrenal gland problems	Runoff from herbicide used on crops

In the United States, the EPA sets national standards for safe drinking water. For dozens of substances, the EPA has determined their maximum contaminant level (MCL); that is, the amount of the contaminant that water can contain and still be safe to drink. Contaminants are measured in terms of milligrams per liter (mg/l) or its equivalent, parts per million (ppm). It may be surprising to learn that drinking water standards include a "safe" level for many substances that are known poisons, such as arsenic and cyanide.

Other institutions, however, have different standards than the EPA for drinking-water quality. The World Health Organization (WHO) also developed a set of guidelines, intended for both developing and developed countries, to set standards and regulations to ensure that drinking water is safe. The WHO's standards are significantly more stringent than the EPA's for the safe levels of cyanide, fluoride, the insecticide endrin, and several other water contaminants. For other substances, the EPA's safety criteria are stricter than the WHO's. Both institutions use rigorous scientific testing to establish their standards. Clearly, even specialized scientists can differ in their test results and the ways in which they interpret their data and define their terminology. If universally accepted standards cannot be established for clean drinking water, certainly it would be difficult to determine the criteria for clean ocean water.

Four

Offshore Oil and Gas Ventures

Oil can enter the oceans via accidents, oily water draining off the land, oily discharges from ships, untreated industrial waste, careless motor oil disposal, and recreational boating. However, as we seek alternatives to fossil fuels (oil, natural gas, and coal), offshore oil production and transport comes into sharp focus.

Offshore Mining

Petroleum and gas are the most economically valuable minerals beneath the ocean floor. The two minerals are often found in the same fuel-rich regions, notably the North Sea, the Gulf of Mexico, and off the coasts of Brazil, Ireland, Nigeria, and many other coastal nations.

Several types of offshore drilling rigs are used for oil and gas mining. A jack-up rig is a platform mounted on a barge. When it reaches the desired location, three or four "legs" are extended down to embed in the seafloor for stability and support. Semi-submersible rigs can drill in much deeper water. They float on pontoons that release air and take in seawater, partially submerging the rig. Huge anchors then hold them in place. Drill ships, which have a drilling platform in the middle of the deck,

A jack-up rig (left) and semisubmersible rig (right) drill for oil in the Caspian Sea.

can operate in very deep water. If exploratory drilling uncovers oil or gas deposits, wellhead equipment is installed over the hole, and a more stable platform is built for extraction. The products are then transported to shore through underwater pipelines or by tanker ships.

The environmental risks of offshore mining include leaks, spills, and blowouts (sudden, uncontrolled eruptions of fluid under high pressure). Many more blowouts happen during exploration than during extraction. Most accidents affect coastal areas because most offshore oil and gas exploration takes place within a country's relatively shallow territorial waters. However, new technologies enable drilling rigs to reach ever greater depths. With oil exploration taking place far from shore, the full effects of accidents on marine life will be difficult to determine.

The Anatomy of an Oil Spill

While oil spills are not the largest source of oil pollution in the oceans, they offer the most dramatic and obvious evidence of oil's environmental impact. Oil spills can result from accidents either in the ocean or on land. A land-based oil refinery or storage facility could explode, or an oil pipeline could burst and send oil into rivers or coastal waters and eventually into the open ocean. An offshore oil rig, whether exploring for oil or pumping it out, could spring a leak. An oil tanker may have an accident that releases its oily contents into the sea.

When oil is released in the water, it first spreads out on the surface, creating an oil slick—a dark patch glistening with rainbowlike colors. Then wind, waves, and currents spread the oil slick over a larger area, possibly breaking it up into separate slicks. As parts of the oil evaporate, what remains becomes thicker and stickier. Depending on the type of oil, it may mix with water and air to form a thick, foamy substance called mousse. (Oil workers sometimes call it "chocolate mousse.") Eventually, the oil breaks apart into "tar balls" that sink or wash ashore. Over time, other oil components degrade, decompose, dissolve, or sink.

In 1989 the *Exxon Valdez* leaked 11 million gallons of oil into the Prince William Sound in Alaska, creating a huge oil slick.

Table 3. Worst Oil Spills at Sea

World

Date	Location	Source	Cause	Gallons of Oil[a]
1991	Persian Gulf, off Kuwait	Oil tankers	Deliberate release	240–460 million
2010	Gulf of Mexico, off Louisiana, USA	*Deepwater Horizon* (exploratory rig)	Blowout	205.8 million (est.)[b]
1979	Bay of Campeche, Mexico	*Ixtoc I* (exploratory rig)	Blowout	140 million
1983	Nowruz Oil Field, Persian Gulf, off Iran	Two oil platforms	(Tanker-platform collision; bombing	80 million
1979	Caribbean Sea, off Tobago	*Atlantic Empress, Aegean Captain* (oil tankers)	Collision of two ships	46 million on collision plus 41 million during towing

[a]Oil volume is often given in barrels. One barrel = 42 gallons; 1 gallon = .0238 barrels.

[b]Or 4.9 million barrels, per the Flow Rate Technical Group (FRTG), August 2, 2010.

Sources: Oil Spills and Disasters, Infoplease, www.infoplease.com/ipa/A0001451.html; "Federal Science Report Details Fate of Oil from BP Spill," Restore the Gulf, August 4, 2010, http://app.restorethegulf.gov/go/doc/2931/846739/; *Nowruz Oil Field*, NOAA, www.incidentnews.gov/incident/6262; Exxon Valdez Oil Spill Trustee Council, www.evostc.state.ak.us/facts/qanda.cfm (accessed August 6, 2010).

Through a process called biodegradation, various types of bacteria and other microorganisms can break down the components of crude oil into water and carbon dioxide, but the practical aspects of this operation are problematic. One problem is the difficulty of amassing enough of these organisms to make a real impact on a large oil spill. Usually a consortium, or combination, of two or more types of microorganisms is needed for successful biodegradation. Some of these organisms live naturally in the marine environment. Others must be produced by scientists on a large scale in a lab. Another problem is the time it takes to degrade the oil. Some oil components are processed in the early stages of biodegradation, while other components resist biodegradation and thus take longer to process. Wind and waves, temperature, water salinity and acidity, and the presence or absence of oxygen and other nutrients affect the speed with which microorganisms will process the oil.

Oil spills have a devastating impact on marine life. Dead fish and shellfish wash up on shore as the oil cuts off their

A brown pelican is coated in oil as a result of the 2010 *Deepwater Horizon* blowout and explosion, which released millions of gallons of oil into the Gulf of Mexico.

oxygen supply or poisons them. Marine birds and mammals, coated with oil, flop around helplessly. As the slick spreads out into the ocean and thins out, it may not be apparent that oil continues to affect marine life. However, organisms that survive an oil spill are dangerously contaminated, and their metabolisms are disrupted. When fish are exposed to oil, they grow more slowly, their livers enlarge, their heart rate changes, their fins erode, and they do not reproduce as well as usual. Shellfish such as clams and oysters experience similar symptoms. The oil these creatures absorb enters the food chain and is eventually eaten by humans. Besides being a health hazard, oil spills can have a severe impact on those whose livelihoods depend on fishing.

Managing an Oil Spill

Preventing an oil spill is the best management strategy, of course, and offshore wellheads are equipped with emergency shutoff valves called blowout preventers. But once a spill happens, the environmental damage must be minimized and stopped. A wellhead that keeps gushing oil must be capped, a difficult and dangerous maneuver. Meanwhile, a cleanup must begin as quickly as possible to catch the spreading oil.

In the United States, both the Coast Guard and the Environmental Protection Agency (EPA) investigate and respond to oil contamination incidents. Which agency takes the lead in cleaning up oil spills depends on where the spill occurs. For most oil spills at sea, it would be the Coast Guard, which is responsible for contamination in all U.S. coastal zones, offshore waters, the Great Lakes, and deepwater ports. The EPA, on the other hand, is mainly responsible for pollution on land and inland waters. In case of a Spill of National Significance (SONS), federal, state, and local agencies—including the EPA and the National Oceanic and Atmospheric Administration (NOAA), all the way down to local fire departments and citizen volunteers—coordinate their efforts.

Cleanup crews first try to contain the oil slick with a boom—a long, narrow barrier that floats on the surface and has a skirt hanging down into the water to stop the oil. They may drag the

The *Deepwater Horizon* Disaster

On the night of April 20, 2010, in the Gulf of Mexico, off the Louisiana coast, a blowout triggered a massive explosion and fire aboard the oil rig *Deepwater Horizon*. The disaster left eleven people dead and unleashed the largest offshore oil spill in U.S. history. Crude oil spread over thousands of square miles of the Gulf, threatening fisheries and wildlife in the region's coastal waters and fragile wetlands.

Deepwater Horizon, a semisubmersible exploratory rig, was operating under contract to the British energy company BP. The rig's blowout preventer failed to shut off the oil flow, so that hundreds of thousands of gallons of oil gushed into the Gulf every day. BP tried several techniques to stop the flow, including lowering domes to contain the oil and injecting heavyweight mud to seal the well. All operations were done with remotely operated machinery, as the wellhead was 5,000 feet (1,524 m) underwater—almost a mile down, too deep for human divers to survive the water pressure.

Finally, on July 15, almost three months after the explosion, BP was able to cap the wellhead. The millions of gallons of oil already released into the Gulf had reached the coastal areas of not only Louisiana but also Texas, Mississippi, Alabama, and Florida. It will take years to assess the spill's full impact on the environment, fisheries, tourism, the oil industry, and global energy policies.

boom through the water by boat, surround an inlet to keep the oil out, or position the boom along the coastline to protect the beach. In case of a leaking oil tanker, crews surround it with booms to contain the oil.

Once the oil is confined within an area, it can be removed using skimmers. Suction skimmers suck the oil into storage tanks; adhesion skimmers use belts, drums, or discs made of oil-absorbing material to soak up the oil like sponges and deposit it into a container. These containers may be on board a ship, or the oil may be sent by pipeline to containers on the shore.

Sometimes oil dispersants are used to treat oil spills. Dispersants are chemical detergents that break the oil down into smaller droplets that certain marine bacteria can decompose. This treatment is not ideal, though, because both the dispersants and the oil droplets are toxic to other marine organisms. Also, in testing the effects of oil dispersants on coral reefs, scientists have found that the dispersants and the droplets cause the corals more stunted growth and deaths than crude oil.

Wildlife Recovery after an Oil Spill

The largest wildlife recovery effort in U.S. history took place in 1989 after the oil tanker *Exxon Valdez* spilled about 11 million gallons of oil into the pristine waters of Alaska's Prince William Sound. In the first few weeks after the spill, recovery workers picked up the oil-covered carcasses of about 35,000 seabirds and 1,000 sea otters. Most carcasses sink, though, so actual deaths are estimated at 250,000 seabirds, 2,800 sea otters, 300 harbor seals, 250 bald eagles, and as many as 22 killer whales. Billions of fish eggs were destroyed, too.

On fur-bearing marine mammals such as sea otters, the fur insulates their bodies from cold water and air. A coating of oil removes the fur's insulating properties. Seabirds' feathers have a similar function, serving as a water repellent and as insulation. Without these protective mechanisms, their body temperature drops, and they die of hypothermia. Also, birds and mammals coated with the oil try to clean themselves and in the process consume the oil and die of poisoning. Thus, oil-spill recovery

Renewable Energy Facilities

Extracting fossil fuels is one way to draw energy resources from the sea. However, the oceans offer many opportunities to produce energy in renewable ways. For example, Denmark, Sweden, the United Kingdom, and other countries are currently operating offshore wind farms. Canada, France, and Northern Ireland have hydroelectric plants powered by tidal energy. Offshore solar power plants, now in the experimental stage, are potential energy sources as well.

Wave farms, another ocean-based energy resource, harness the energy in ocean waves to generate electricity. In 2008, Portugal became the first nation to operate a commercial wave farm when it opened the Aguçadora Wave Farm off the country's northern coast. Scotland launched a similar system in 2010, and other countries are currently developing wave energy plans. In the United States, the Department of Energy is funding research and development of wave energy technology.

efforts involve the laborious process of cleaning marine birds and mammals individually to remove the oil.

After the *Exxon Valdez* spill, dozens of biologists, veterinarians, rehab specialists, and volunteers worked to save surviving but severely oiled seabirds, bald eagles, and sea otters. First they captured the animals using long-handled nets. Then they warmed them in towels and gave them fluids to prevent dehydration. In Seward, Alaska, the International Bird Rescue Research Center (IBRRC) set up a rehabilitation facility for captured birds. There workers washed the birds in soapy water, rinsed them thoroughly, and let them rest and dry. There were large cages where eagles could practice flying again and pools where seabirds could practice swimming. Once a bird seemed fully recovered, it was released into the wild. Sea otters received similar treatments.

Oil spills can continue to affect wildlife for decades. Alaska wildlife officials are studying species affected by the oil spill to see which populations have returned to their prespill level. They reported that, in 2010, populations of Barrow's goldeneyes

Animal rescue workers wash an oil-soaked sea otter in Valdez, Alaska, in 1989.

(sea ducks), harlequin ducks, black oystercatchers (seabirds), clams, sea otters, and a resident pod (feeding troop) of killer whales were still recovering. Populations of Pacific herring, pigeon guillemots (seabirds), and another killer whale pod were not recovering and continuing to decline. Studies of harlequin ducks living in the area show that they were still ingesting oil residue in 2009, twenty years after the spill. Needless to say, commercial fishing and Alaska Natives' subsistence harvests have not yet recovered either.

Oil companies hope to minimize the environmental impacts of oil spills. In 2007, an Exxon spokesperson claimed, "it is clear that there have been no effects on the environment that remain ecologically significant." However, it seems that oil lingers in the water for much longer periods than even scientists had thought. According to NOAA chemist Jeffrey Short, "We expected the natural decay rate was 25% a year. But very little of the oil actually disappeared." Instead, the oil is decaying at a rate of 3 to 4 percent a year. These figures have grim implications for the 2010 *Deepwater Horizon* incident, as well as for oil spills around the world.

Five
Fisheries in Crisis

Fishing is the most obvious ocean-based economic activity. People in many coastal areas make their living by fishing, and fish and shellfish make up a major part of their diet. In fact, about one billion people worldwide rely on fish as their main source of animal protein. In terms of fishing as an economic activity, the largest segment of world fisheries is commercial fishing. Commercial fishers range from the small, one-person rowboats that go out for a day at a time to huge fishing fleets that spend weeks on an expedition.

Fish caught include salmon, tuna, shellfish (lobsters, shrimp, and crabs), and other edible species such as squid. Consumers are used to buying these seafoods in grocery stores, restaurants, and village markets around the world. Yet, the supply is not infinite. As the world's population swells, the demand for fishing products puts intense pressure on fish populations. The worldwide catch of ocean fish swelled from 20 million tons in 1950 to 81 million tons in 2003. Even nonfood species are threatened because many of today's common fishing methods result in some degree of bycatch. That is the unintended capture of creatures other than the target species.

Fishing Methods

Common commercial fishing methods vary in their efficiency and collateral damage. Many fishing fleets use the long-lining method. It involves stringing out long fishing lines with baited hooks. Longlines are often strung between buoys and weighted to reach a certain depth, from near-surface to seafloor. They range in length from a few hundred feet to several miles. A negative impact of long-lining is that seabirds and other marine creatures go for the bait, get caught, and drown. Trolling is similar to long-lining, only the baited lines are strung behind a boat that's moving slowly through the water.

For groundfish such as cod and halibut, fishers use bottom trawling, a method that involves dragging large, weighted nets along the seafloor. This method damages the seafloor, upsets its habitats, and catches corals, sponges, turtles, sharks, and many other marine species. Shrimp are another species commonly captured by bottom trawling.

Seining is a method of surrounding fish that swim in schools, such as sardines. The seine is a large, round net that

A commercial fishing vessel pulls in seine gear laden with salmon.

is weighted so it forms a bowl shape in the water. Fish swim in, and the fisher hauls up a net full of fish. A purse seine has a wire running around the edge so that the net can be pulled shut like a drawstring bag.

Gill netting involves long "walls" of fishnet suspended vertically in the water. The fish are caught when their gills get stuck in the netting. Other methods include traditional pole-and-line fishing, as well as trapping, where fish or shellfish swim into a container and cannot get out.

Impacts of Overfishing

The major impact of overfishing is a decline in fish populations. According to a group of prominent marine biologists, "80% of the world's fish stocks are either fully exploited, overexploited or have collapsed." Tuna, for example, is one of the most commercially valuable fish in the world, with many desirable species in the world's oceans. Most canned tuna in the United States is albacore tuna. The only seafoods that outnumber tuna sales are shrimp and groundfish (bottom-dwellers such as sole, halibut, and flounder). Among the major commercial tuna species, most are dangerously overfished. Their populations are monitored by the International Union for Conservation of Nature (IUCN).

The IUCN ranks thousands of animals and plants on its Red List of Threatened Species. Those considered threatened may be ranked as vulnerable, endangered, or critically endangered, depending on their risk of extinction. The IUCN has placed seven stocks, or regional supplies, of tuna on its Red List (see Table 4, p. 54). Other Red List fish include Atlantic halibut (endangered), Atlantic cod (vulnerable), and red grouper (near threatened).

Another casualty of commercial fishing is the bycatch. These accidental catches include sharks, sea turtles, dolphins, and even seabirds. Critically injured or dead when they are hauled in, bycatch species are routinely dumped overboard. Researchers estimate that one-fourth of the world's annual catch is discarded this way, amounting to 20 million tons of bycatch a year. Bottom trawling for shrimp is the most

Table 4. Status of Tuna Species

Tuna Species	Region	IUCN Status
Albacore	North Atlantic	Vulnerable
Albacore	South Atlantic	Critically endangered
Bigeye	South and Central Atlantic	Vulnerable
Bigeye	Pacific	Endangered
Northern bluefin	Eastern Atlantic	Endangered
Northern bluefin	Western Atlantic	Critically endangered
Southern bluefin	South Atlantic, Indian Ocean, southwest Pacific	Critically endangered

Source: IUCN 2010. "The IUCN Red List of Threatened Species," version 2010.1, www.iucnredlist.org/ (accessed April 9, 2010).

environmentally costly. For every pound of shrimp caught, another 3 to 15 pounds of other marine organisms are wasted as bycatch. In fact, shrimp trawling accounts for more than 25 percent of the world's bycatch every year.

Contaminants

Contaminants are another environmental hazard affecting the fishing industry. According to the UN environmental agency Earthwatch, "direct dumping [of wastes] at sea is one of the fastest ways for toxic compounds to enter the food chain." Many fish and shellfish have been found to contain harmful substances such as mercury, dioxins, and polychlorinated biphenyls (PCBs). They enter the oceans as by-products of various industrial processes. Traces of mercury are found in almost all fish products. Those with high levels of mercury are shark, swordfish, king mackerel, and tilefish. According to the Food and Drug Administration (FDA), young children

A trapped sea turtle becomes an accidental catch, known to commercial fishermen as "bycatch."

and pregnant women should avoid eating these fish. Tuna generally has a low mercury content, but albacore has higher mercury levels than canned light tuna.

Contamination of fish, crabs, clams, oysters, mussels, and shrimp is also a hazard when oil spills occur near a coastal fishing area. During these emergencies, state wildlife and health agencies test local species for the presence of oil contaminants and may announce fishing closures, or bans on fishing. Bans were imposed after both the 1989 *Exxon Valdez* oil spill in Alaskan waters and the 2010 *Deepwater Horizon* oil spill in the Gulf of Mexico.

As more chemical contaminants enter the oceans, the concern about the health aspects of eating contaminated fish and shellfish may lead to decreased fish consumption. However, fish and shellfish contain high-quality proteins, are low in calories and saturated fat, and are major sources of omega-3 fatty acids and iodine, essential to human nutrition. A study in the Netherlands showed that the health risks from eating fish and

other foods that may contain chemical contaminants were in fact up to one hundred times lower than the risks of eating foods that are high in saturated fats.

Aquaculture—A Sustainable Solution

One way of sustaining the oceans' natural fish stocks is aquaculture—the raising of fish, shellfish, and aquatic plants on farms. Aquaculture facilities range in size from small family farms to huge corporate operations. In the European Union (EU), aquaculture accounts for almost one-fifth of the fishing industry's entire production. About half the seafood eaten in the United States comes from fish farms. That figure mirrors the farmed fish consumption worldwide. According to the UN's Food and Agriculture Organization (FAO), aquaculture now accounts for nearly 50 percent of the world's food fish.

Aquaculture farms around the world raise hundreds of species. About half the world's aquaculture consists of species raised in freshwater and brackish (slightly salty) water. The other half of the industry involves marine species. Salmon, bass, cod, and sea bream are some of the commonly farmed ocean fish. Farmed shellfish include oysters, mussels, clams, and crabs. As for shrimp, typically raised in coastal farms and tanks, some countries classify them as brackish species, and others consider them marine organisms. A large percentage of marine aquaculture involves kelp (or seaweed, a type of algae with a high nutritional value) and other aquatic plants.

Aquaculturists use a variety of methods to raise their stock. Some aquaculture farms are located in an ocean lagoon or just off the coast; they use fences, nets, or cages to contain the stock. Other farms raise aquatic species in huge tanks of water. Flow-through tanks are built to let water pass naturally into and out of the system, while recirculation tanks, which are closed, filter and reuse the water. Recirculation tanks are ideal systems for assuring that the organisms are free from contaminants. As grown fish are harvested for sale, new hatchlings add to the stock; eggs or young fish may also be introduced to increase the population. Fish farms are highly productive because they protect their species from predators. While fish in the wild

Aquaculturists raise Atlantic salmon on this "farm" in New Brunswick, Canada.

scavenge for whatever they can find, farmed fish are typically fed with clean, nutritious food. However, on many farms that raise oysters, clams, and mussels, these shellfish are left to draw nutrients from their environment without any outside input.

As environmentally friendly as aquaculture seems, it does have some drawbacks. Some farm-raised species are carnivores; their diet consists of other fish. Every year, tons of wild fish such as sardines and anchovies are processed into fishmeal and fish oil to feed to farm-raised fish. A farmed salmon, for example, must consume more than three pounds of fish to gain one pound of weight. Researchers are currently trying to find healthful food substitutes for carnivorous fish. Another issue is the use of antibiotics and other chemicals in farm-raised fish to prevent or cure diseases. Residue from these drugs can remain in the fish and get passed on to humans. Aquaculturists in Norway and several other countries address this problem by vaccinating their farm-raised fish. Some countries have strict regulations about what imported fish have been fed, and many drugs are banned for use in aquaculture. The FAO, World

Health Organization (WHO), and other groups are working to get aquaculture antibiotics banned altogether.

Fisheries Management Issues

Although there are international and local restrictions on overfishing, the practice continues and is even escalating. Several factors are at work here. Some countries that have pledged to honor international fishing regulations simply do not do so, and methods of detecting violations and enforcing regulations are weak. Only a handful of countries have systematic, well-managed, science-based fishing controls in place.

Another factor is that some governments give subsidies to their fishers to help them stay in business. As a result, dwindling fish catches do not discourage them from continuing to fish and overexploit the fish stocks. In addition, some developing countries routinely sell fishing rights in their waters to industrialized nations, which may then disregard catch limits or bycatch restrictions.

These and other fishing abuses come under the umbrella term of illegal, unreported, and unregulated (IUU) fishing. These practices exhaust fish supplies, destroy marine habitats, make for unfair competition, and put honest fishers at an unfair disadvantage. IUU fishing also weakens costal communities, especially in developing countries. Ideally, these weaknesses in fisheries management systems can be reduced through regional and international pressure and a growing awareness of global responsibility.

A Model of Fisheries Management

The EU provides an excellent model for fisheries management. It has been aggressively overseeing its fishing fleets for decades. EU marine fisheries encompass four major regions—the Baltic Sea, the northeastern Atlantic Ocean, the Mediterranean Sea, and the Black Sea. In 1983 the EU established the Common Fisheries Policy (CFP) and radically reformed the policy in 2002. Under the new version, the CFP has rules to ensure that the EU's fisheries are sustainable and do not damage marine ecosystems and the marine environment. Policies are aimed at

Overfishing has become a practice that is severely affecting the ocean's fish stocks.

Fishing for Products and Cures

Fishing for food is just one reason for pursuing marine life. Another thriving ocean-based activity is bioprospecting—the search for plant or animal species that can be used in making new medicines and other products. It is hard to say whether bioprospecting is scientific research or a commercial activity, as the two efforts are rarely completely separate. As of 2006, more than a dozen commercial companies were collaborating with research institutions to find new chemical compounds from marine organisms. Products derived from deep-sea creatures range from possible anticancer drugs to skin-care products and antifreeze.

protecting the ecological balance in EU waters. Perhaps most important, the CFP provides national authorities with the tools to enforce its rules and punish offenders.

CFP officials monitor the EU fishing fleet. This monitoring involves not only restricting the size of each country's fleet but also limiting the number of days a fleet can spend out at sea. Other rules put a ceiling on the quantity of fish that can be taken in before fishers must stop fishing. The CFP sets limits, called total allowable catches (TACs), on the most common commercial fish species in European waters. Each country is given annual quotas on most species and biennial TACs for deep-sea species. As CFP scientists monitor the stocks of each species, quotas are adjusted upward or downward, maintaining a fair ratio among the various countries' limits.

These quotas are partly responsible for the common practice among EU fishers of throwing their unwanted bycatch back into the water while still at sea. The discarded bycatch would otherwise be counted toward a fleet's fishing quota when the total catch is weighed. Authorities are also encouraging fishers to develop more selective fishing methods to reduce the amount of netted bycatch. Another plan under consideration is to temporarily close fishing areas that have a high concentration of fish that should not be caught, such as young fish or threatened species.

Not everyone is happy with the quota system. Fishers in some member states feel that the quotas are crippling their fishing industry. One Scottish fisherman complained, "In 30 years at sea I have never caught a whale, destroyed a dolphin, or dumped nuclear waste, but I have been forced by the EU to dump hundreds of tonnes of edible fish in the name of 'euro-conservation'." Scotland's World Wildlife Fund representative points out that "current policies are failing to conserve fish stocks and sustain jobs for communities." Realizing that there are deep-rooted problems with the current policies, the EU Fisheries Commission began yet another overhaul of the CFP. Among the revisions under discussion in 2010 were making changes in the quota system and giving member states more regional control over their own fisheries.

The EU Common Fisheries Policy oversees the size of the EU fishing fleet, such as those in Spain (above).

In 2010 the EU introduced stern measures to combat illegal, unreported, and unregulated fishing. One new regulation is that only fishing products validated as legal can be imported into or exported from the EU. A public blacklist of IUU offenders has been drawn up, too. It covers both individual fishing vessels and those states that choose to ignore illegal fishing activities. EU fishers who operate illegally anywhere in the world face stiff fines depriving them of any profit from their catches. The EU has agreements with many developing countries that allow them access to fish in their waters. However, after the CFP was revamped, these relationships were changed to partnerships for developing responsible fisheries. All these measures are aimed at creating sustainable fisheries both within EU waters and beyond them.

Six

Oceans and the Law

In his 1968 article "The Tragedy of the Commons," biologist Garrett Hardin offered a disparaging view of humans' ability to work for the common good. When people share a common resource that benefits them all, he says, they will eventually destroy that resource because humans naturally try to maximize their individual gain. "Freedom in a commons brings ruin to all," says Hardin. The only way to avert the ruin is to pass "coercive laws." Hardin's assessment may be harsh; nevertheless, laws have gone a long way toward preserving the "commons" of the oceans.

International shipping, including the oil trade, grew tremendously in the first half of the twentieth century. It was a routine practice for ships to discharge oily substances from their machinery spaces into the open sea. Many countries introduced regulations to control the discharge of these wastes in their territorial waters. However, the problem was not addressed on a global scale until the mid–twentieth century.

OILPOL and MARPOL

In 1954 the United Kingdom organized an international conference on oil pollution. The result was the International Convention for the Prevention of Pollution of the Sea by

Oil (OILPOL)—the first international agreement on ocean pollution. The International Maritime Organization (IMO), an agency of the United Nations, was given the authority to oversee it. Signed in 1954, OILPOL went into effect in 1958. It set up prohibited zones, forbidding oil discharges within 50 miles of land, and required shippers to have facilities to receive their oily water. Amendments in 1969 added more restrictions.

In 1967 the tanker *Torrey Canyon* ran aground in the English Channel, spilling all its contents into the sea. This incident raised the question of environmental disasters caused by accidental spills and the issue of compensation for damages inflicted by these spills. By this time, it had become clear that there were many other ways for ships to harm the environment than by discharging oil. So the IMO called another conference to draw up a more sweeping agreement. Adopted in 1973 and amended in 1978, it had a very long name—International Convention for the Prevention of Pollution from Ships, 1973, as modified

The tanker *Torrey Canyon* breaks apart after hitting rocks and spilling huge quantities of crude oil into the sea.

by the Protocol of 1978 relating thereto. This agreement came to be known as MARPOL 73/78, or just MARPOL—short for "marine pollution."

MARPOL has six annexes, or technical divisions, each dealing with a different type of pollution. These six divisions, as numbered, address (I) oil, (II) toxic liquid chemicals, (III) harmful packaged substances, (IV) sewage, (V) garbage, and (VI) air pollution. Each signatory country was required to adopt at least the first two annexes and also to pass national laws in support of MARPOL's provisions. As of October 2010, 150 countries had adopted the first two annexes. Those countries account for 99.14 percent of the world's shipping tonnage. Signers of the remaining annexes represent more than 80 percent of international shipping.

The London Convention

MARPOL was designed to guard against both routine pollution (operational pollution) and accidental pollution by ships. However, it did not address the important issue of dumping—the practice of carrying wastes from land out into the ocean with the sole purpose of disposing of them. Specialized dumping vessels had been hauling wastes out to sea for years. They dumped industrial by-products, chemical sludge, sewage sludge, barrels of radioactive wastes, and other substances. Incineration ships were sailing into the open ocean and burning wastes, polluting both the air and sea.

To deal with this problem, the IMO drew up another international agreement: the Convention on the Prevention of Marine Pollution by Dumping of Wastes and Other Matter 1972, commonly called the London Convention or the London Dumping Convention. It was modernized and updated in 1996 by the London Protocol, which overlaps and will eventually replace the 1972 agreement.

In addition to the usual wastes, the London Protocol regulates the disposal of a surprising variety of materials: oil-drilling platforms, spoiled meat and crops, fish wastes from industrial fish processing, sediments dredged from the seafloor, mining wastes, and construction materials such as iron, steel, and concrete.

The Law of the Sea

While the IMO was developing antipollution agreements, the United Nations was drawing up international laws governing the oceans. These laws would replace the centuries-old "freedom of the seas" model. Law of the Sea conferences were held from 1956 to 1958, in 1960, and from 1973 to 1982, arriving at a final version in 1982. The UN Convention on the Law of the Sea (UNCLOS), or Law of the Sea Convention (LOSC), finally went into effect in 1994.

UNCLOS's legal definitions became international standards. A coastal nation's territorial waters extend 12 nautical miles (13.8 miles) from its baseline, or low-water mark. A nation may set its own laws for this area and has exclusive use of the resources there, including fisheries and oil exploration. The exclusive economic zone (EEZ) extends beyond the territorial waters 200 nautical miles (230 miles) from the baseline or else to the end of the continental shelf, whichever distance is farther. Here, too, a nation has sole rights to the resources. Beyond the EEZ is the open ocean, or high seas. All nations have a right to resources in the high seas.

A nation's territorial waters extend 12 nautical miles from shore. Each nation sets its own set of usage laws for these waters, including fishing.

UNCLOS also reinforces all the antipollution measures of the IMO conventions, and it adds stricter ways to enforce the rules. Under UNCLOS, a port nation may bring legal proceedings against shippers that pollute its ports and also shippers that have committed any act of pollution at sea.

Many coastal countries have also drawn up regional antipollution conventions. They include the Helsinki (Finland) Convention for states along the Baltic Sea, the Paris (France) Convention for states on the northern Atlantic, the Barcelona (Spain) Convention for the Mediterranean Sea, and the Lima (Peru) Convention for the southeastern Pacific Ocean.

Oil Spills, Land-Based Discharges, and Fisheries

As other ocean management issues continued to surface, the international community rose to the occasion by urging broad agreements among oil-shipping nations. For example, as oil spills in the marine environment became more frequent and more severe, the IMO drew up the International Convention on Oil Pollution Preparedness, Response and Cooperation, 1990 (OPRC 90). It requires ships to report incidents of oil pollution and to have an emergency action plan in case of spills.

Pollution at sea is only part of the problem, since most ocean pollution comes from land-based activities. Concerned about the effects of land-based pollution on marine biodiversity and ecosystems, the UN Environment Programme (UNEP) instituted the Global Program of Action for the Protection of the Marine Environment from Land-Based Activities (GPA) in 1995. Its member nations are committed to combating marine pollution from sources such as municipal sewage and solid waste, chemical discharges from factories, fertilizer runoff from farms, and oil spills on land.

Pollutants enter the oceans through the air as well. Gaseous exhaust from airplanes, airborne particles from industrial emissions, and by-products of weapons testing are just some of the materials that drift on the wind and eventually settle in the oceans. Drifting particles can interfere with the hydrologic cycle, too, as they interfere with the formation of rain clouds. These are some of the environmental problems addressed by

Nations worldwide are committed to fighting the problem of pollution at sea.

the Convention on Long-Range Transboundary Air Pollution. The UN Economic Commission for Europe (UNECE) formed this convention in 1979 and has been extending and updating it ever since.

Although the UN's Law of the Sea defined national boundaries for fishing rights, there is little international clout to enforce good fishing practices. The UN's Food and Agriculture Organization (FAO) hoped to address this problem by drawing up the Code of Conduct for Responsible Fisheries in 1995. Its aim was to prevent overfishing and promote long-term, sustainable fisheries, and it encouraged member countries to enact their own national laws for responsible fisheries management. Although many countries signed on to the code and began implementing its guidelines, compliance was purely voluntary.

U.S. Ocean Protection Laws

The United States has passed several laws to help combat ocean pollution. One is the Federal Water Pollution Control Act of 1972, usually called the Clean Water Act (CWA). It bans the release of a variety of pollutants into U.S. territorial waters. In order to discharge wastes into the water, a city or industrial plant has to obtain a National Pollutant Discharge Elimination System (NPDES) permit. Getting that permit requires treating the wastes to meet stringent water quality and safety standards. However, the CWA does not ban the discharge of raw sewage from cruise ships and other vessels.

The Marine Protection, Research, and Sanctuaries Act of 1972 (also called the Ocean Dumping Act) prohibits transporting wastes with the intention of dumping them in U.S. waters. The act covers materials such as sewage, medical wastes, radioactive wastes, and nuclear, biological, and chemical weapons.

The Oil Pollution Prevention, Response, Liability, and Compensation Act, or just Oil Pollution Act (OPA), targets oil spills. Congress enacted it in response to the 1989 *Exxon Valdez* oil spill in Alaska. The OPA imposes liability on any party responsible for an oil spill within the nation's EEZ. That party must pay for all cleanup costs and damages. The act establishes an oil spill liability trust fund that can be used immediately in case of an oil spill. It also requires oil tankers to have double hulls to minimize the possibility of leaks through cracked or damaged hulls.

The Coastal Zone Management Act recognizes the fragile ecosystems of fish, shellfish, and other wildlife in coastal areas. It requires coastal states to manage their pollution sources and grants them federal funds to create pollution-management programs.

To protect marine species, the United States enacted the Marine Mammal Protection Act of 1972 (MMPA). It protects marine mammals such as whales, dolphins, porpoises, sea lions, seals, and sea otters, as well as other animals that depend on the marine environment, including manatees, sea otters, and polar bears. Under the MMPA, it is unlawful "to harass, hunt, capture, or kill, or attempt to harass, hunt, capture, or kill" these animals. (Native peoples who kill these animals for subsistence are exempt.)

69

Federal Oversight Agencies

Besides marine protection laws, the United States has several federal agencies that monitor the coastal and marine environment. The Environmental Protection Agency (EPA) includes an Office of Wetlands, Oceans and Watersheds. Within that office, the Oceans and Coastal Protection Division monitors water quality and enforces regulations on marine pollution, marine debris, ocean dumping, and dredged material.

The U.S. Coast Guard plays an important role in protecting the marine environment, too. It makes sure foreign ships do not pollute U.S. waters, and its Environmental Standards Division develops antipollution guidelines for industries, states, and the public. In case of an oil spill in U.S. waters, the Coast Guard is the lead agency in overseeing response efforts. The Coast Guard was the overseer in the two most disastrous U.S. oil spills: the 2010 *Deepwater Horizon* spill in the Gulf of Mexico and the 1989 *Exxon Valdez* spill in Prince William Sound, Alaska.

The Marine Mammal Protection Act was created to protect marine mammals such as manatees.

The National Oceanic and Atmospheric Administration (NOAA) is an agency of the U.S. Department of Commerce. Some of NOAA's many science-oriented divisions are the National Ocean Service and the Office of Ocean Exploration and Research. NOAA's Office of Ocean and Coastal Resource Management (OCRM) conserves natural resources in coastal areas. It also oversees more than 1,600 marine protected areas (MPAs) within U.S. waters. NOAA is the main federal agency working on the Integrated Ocean Observing System (IOOS). This information-gathering network collects data on oceans from the global level down to the local level so that scientists can examine changes in the marine environment.

Several other U.S. government departments have a hand in preventing and managing marine pollution. For example, the Bureau of Ocean Energy Management, Regulation and Enforcement (BOEMRE; formerly the Minerals Management Service) is a bureau of the U.S. Department of the Interior. It manages the nation's offshore oil, natural gas, and other mineral resources. The Department of State's Bureau of Oceans and International Environmental and Scientific Affairs takes a global approach to biodiversity, climate change, and pollution issues.

Many U.S. agencies form their marine policies in conjunction with international guidelines. This policy allows for better collaboration with other countries on ocean issues that cross national boundaries. Also, whereas international conventions cannot always enforce ocean policies, national governments can. Agencies worldwide encourage industries and private citizens to go beyond the law and take a proactive approach to ocean management.

Seven

Proactive Strategies for a Global Resource

Without a doubt, there are plenty of laws and regulations in place for protecting the oceans from misuse by humans. Offenders are punished with warnings, reprimands, restrictions, penalties, fines, and negative publicity. It would be ideal if everyone who uses the oceans were inspired not by fear but by a global vision of long-term sustainability. Such a vision would generate positive, proactive, forward-looking ways to achieve both economic and environmental goals.

Fortunately, many ocean-management practices do raise public awareness about marine resources. Other procedures induce project managers to consider environmental impacts early in the planning process and to make conservation a part of doing business. Many of these strategies are already being applied, though unevenly, and they need to be expanded.

Environmental Impact Assessments
Underwater construction, mineral exploration, equipment testing, seafloor surveys, research projects, and many other operations are going on in the oceans all the time. To preserve

the marine ecosystem, it is essential that project managers make environmental impact assessments (EIAs) before they begin and include plans for minimizing their impact on the ocean environment.

EIAs often involve soliciting the public for comments, suggestions, and possible collaborations. The public includes companies, environmental organizations, and ordinary people whose interests could be affected by a given project. If a project in the waters of one city, county, state, or country could have an impact on the waters in another jurisdiction, those entities need to be notified and consulted.

International agreements already require EIAs for certain activities. For example, the UN Fish Stocks Agreement requires its members, when fishing for one species, to assess the impact of their fisheries on other species that share the same ecosystem. For dumping certain kinds of wastes, the London Protocol grants a dumping permit only after the dumper outlines what kind of waste it is, the ecology of the proposed dump site, the waste's effect on the ecosystem, and the method of disposal. The Law of the Sea Convention (LOSC) requires member countries to assess planned projects in terms of their potential for pollution and for significant changes to the marine environment. The UN Convention on Biological Diversity (CBD) directs members to assess their projects from the viewpoint of making as little negative impact as possible.

Many countries have also enacted national laws requiring EIAs. In the United States, environmental impact statements are required for large projects such as building roads and dams and drilling for oil and gas. Many individual states also require environmental assessments for local projects such as housing developments and shopping centers. Coastal states are especially vigilant about projects planned near the shore or in coastal waters.

Having a law on the books, however, does not mean that law is enforced. More than seventy developing countries have enacted EIA legislation, although many of them did so because of outside pressure. EIAs cost money, and developing countries may not see EIAs as a priority in the face of social and

Countries around the world are concerned about construction projects along their coastal waters and many have enacted laws to protect the coastal environment.

economic development projects that need financing. Developing countries may not have environmental experts on hand to conduct EIA studies and may not have data from earlier years for comparison. Literacy problems may prevent consultations with the community and dissemination of information. In addition, governments in these countries may not be accustomed to open and transparent processes. Some of these problems occur even in the United States, when corrupt officials accept bribes and payoffs and make secret agreements.

Hard Choices: Hearing All Sides of a Debate

Scientists on both sides of hotly debated issues need the freedom to air their arguments. One difficult aspect of ocean management is evaluating the tradeoffs—weighing the relative merits and disadvantages of a given strategy. This problem is apparent in ocean-based operations aimed at reducing

Undersea Research

Scientists conduct undersea research for a variety of purposes. They study the ocean to understand its processes, investigate pollution, learn about marine habitats, measure ocean temperatures, map the ocean floor, and discover new species. Many of these operations have little impact on the marine environment. However, scientists still need to assess their environmental impact before undertaking large-scale activities, research on fragile ecosystems, and activities that introduce new substances into the water. Noise pollution is also a danger when using sonar and other acoustic systems. Excess underwater noise can disrupt the communication, migration, and mating habits of whales and other marine mammals.

the amount of carbon dioxide (CO_2) in the atmosphere. Even for those projects, which are designed to improve the environment, international organizations have decided that the environmental impact could be harmful and that further study is required.

For example, open-ocean iron fertilization involves dumping iron into ocean water to stimulate the growth of algae and other phytoplankton that take in CO_2 as they grow. This increased uptake of CO_2 is believed to be one way to decrease the excess CO_2 in the atmosphere. However, some studies have shown that iron fertilization also stimulates the growth of organisms that emit toxins. LOSC officials have decided that the impact of iron fertilization on the marine environment and human health has not yet been determined, and so they currently ban large-scale fertilization projects.

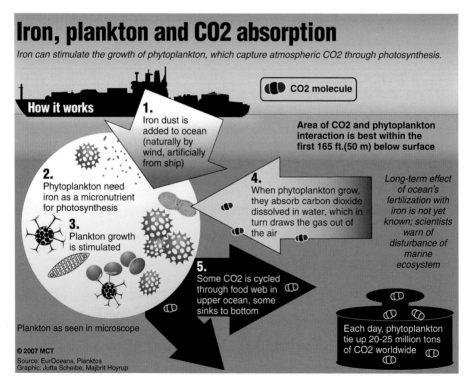

Iron, plankton and CO2 absorption

Iron can stimulate the growth of phytoplankton, which capture atmospheric CO2 through photosynthesis.

CO2 molecule

How it works

1. Iron dust is added to ocean (naturally by wind, artificially from ship)

2. Phytoplankton need iron as a micronutrient for photosynthesis

3. Plankton growth is stimulated

Area of CO2 and phytoplankton interaction is best within the first 165 ft.(50 m) below surface

4. When phytoplankton grow, they absorb carbon dioxide dissolved in water, which in turn draws the gas out of the air

5. Some CO2 is cycled through food web in upper ocean, some sinks to bottom

Long-term effect of ocean's fertilization with iron is not yet known; scientists warn of disturbance of marine ecosystem

Plankton as seen in microscope

© 2007 MCT
Source: EurOceans, Planktos
Graphic: Jutta Scheibe, Majbrit Hoyrup

Each day, phytoplankton tie up 20-25 million tons of CO2 worldwide

This diagram illustrates how iron can stimulate the growth of phytoplankton, which absorbs atmospheric CO_2 through photosynthesis.

Another example is CO_2 sequestration—a term meaning "storage," although that storage is meant to be permanent. The London Protocol has approved CO_2 sequestration in "sub-seabed geological formations." For sequestration, the CO_2 is kept in gaseous form or processed into a highly compressed liquid form called supercritical CO_2. Then it is transported by ship or pipeline to dump sites, which may be undersea pockets of saltwater or oil and gas fields that have been mined out.

Scientists also propose injecting CO_2 directly into the water, where it dissolves. Ships or pipelines would release the CO_2 at depths of 1,000 to 3,000 meters. One problem with this method is that when CO_2 reacts with ocean water, it forms carbonic acid (H_2CO_3), and so the water becomes more acidic. As a result, the metabolisms of deep-sea organisms could be fatally upset because they are unable to absorb oxygen from the acidic water.

In 2002, CO_2 injection experiments were planned off the coasts of Hawaii and Norway. Both were canceled, however, in the face of protests from environmentalist groups and fishing communities. Still, many scientists contend that the net benefit of CO_2 injection—a process that would remove tons of CO_2 that would otherwise be released into the atmosphere—outweighs the possible drawbacks. Nevertheless, the London Protocol has prohibited CO_2 sequestration in ocean water since 1996. However, these and other issues are revisited periodically, and sometimes rulings are changed on the basis of new evidence.

Marine Protected Areas

Establishing marine protected areas (MPAs) is another approach to ocean management geared toward preserving marine ecosystems. These areas typically protect marine plants and animals and their habitats, often including bordering coastal areas and longstanding cultural objects such as bridges and architectural features.

Some MPAs are preserved for scientific research; others are considered wilderness areas or are established to preserve biological diversity. Some allow carefully controlled economic

activities, such as fishing. The International Union for Conservation of Nature (IUCN) has defined six categories of protected areas, each category representing a management objective. Within these categories are hundreds of marine protected areas (see Table 5).

U.S. Marine Protected Areas

There are more than 1,700 marine protected areas throughout the United States and its territories. They are maintained under national, state, or local jurisdiction. MPAs may be in the open ocean, coastal areas, intertidal zones, or estuaries. Some are fragile sites preserved for scientific research, but most are large areas that are open for fishing and recreational use. All, however, are designed to conserve, manage, and protect marine ecosystems. By linking conservation with recreation, these areas have a good chance of delivering an environmental message to the public.

Fourteen of the U.S. MPAs are national marine sanctuaries maintained by the National Oceanic and Atmospheric Administration (NOAA). One is the Florida Keys National Marine Sanctuary, full of coral reefs and sea grass beds. Except for four small research-only areas, visitors are free to go swimming, boating, fishing, and diving to observe underwater life and explore shipwrecks.

The largest national sanctuary is in the middle of the Pacific Ocean. It is the Papahānaumokuākea Marine National Monument, northwest of Hawaii's main islands. This vast underwater sanctuary is one of the largest marine conservation areas in the world. It protects thousands of square miles of island, reef, and deep-sea habitats for species such as the rare green sea turtle and the endangered Hawaiian monk seal.

Monitor National Marine Sanctuary, off the North Carolina coast, was the nation's first MPA. It protects the shipwrecked USS *Monitor*, an ironclad ship that sank during the Civil War. Other U.S. MPAs include Gray's Reef National Marine Sanctuary, off the coast of Georgia, noted for its coral reefs and loggerhead sea turtles; Monterey Bay National Marine Sanctuary, off California's central coast, with underwater canyons

Table 5. Selected International Marine Protected Areas Within IUCN Guidelines

Category	Type	Management Objective	Example
Ia	Strict nature reserve	Science	Union Creek, Bahamas (marine area with sea turtles)
Ib	Wilderness area	Wilderness protection	Archipelago National Park, Finland (rare seals, no-fishing zone)
II	National park	Ecosystem protection and recreation	Bali Barat National Park, Indonesia (includes coral reefs)
III	Natural monument	Conservation of specific natural features	Blue Hole Natural Monument, Belize (deep limestone sinkhole with reef)
IV	Habitat/species management area	Conservation through management intervention	Bandon Marsh National Wildlife Refuge, Oregon (shorebirds)
V	Protected landscape/ seascape	Landscape/seascape conservation and recreation	Great Barrier Reef, Australia (parts are in other categories)
VI	Managed resource protected area	Sustainable use of natural ecosystems	Ulunikoro Marine Reserve, Fiji (locally managed fishing controls)

Source for categories: Protected Areas and World Heritage Programme: Defining Protected Area Management Categories, International Union for Conservation of Nature, 1994, www.unep-wcmc.org/protected_areas/categories/ (accessed May 21, 2010).

Coral and fish thrive at the Papahānaumokuākea Marine
National Monument.

and the nation's largest kelp forest; and Stellwagen Bank
National Marine Sanctuary, in the Gulf of Maine, a famous
whale-watching spot.

Natura 2000: Marine Habitats in the European Union
The European Union's (EU's) plan for marine protected
areas is slightly different from the IUCN's, although the two
share the same goals. The EU drew up the Directive on the
Conservation of Wild Birds (Bird Directive) in 1979 and the
Directive on the Conservation of Natural Habitats and of Wild
Flora and Fauna (Habitats Directive) in 1992. Along with
these directives, ecologists identified 189 types of habitats
and 788 species in the EU that need to be protected. One
measure adopted under the Habitats Directive is a network
of protected areas called Natura 2000. Member states submit
sites for evaluation; after acceptance into the Natura 2000

network, the states actively manage the sites to protect their habitats and animal species.

Under this plan, nine types of marine habitat were identified as needing protection: subtidal sandbanks, estuaries, intertidal mudflats and sandflats, coastal lagoons, large shallow inlets and bays, reefs, Posidonia beds (sea-grass meadows), submarine structures made by leaking gases, and submerged or partially submerged sea caves.

One of the Natura 2000 sites is Ses Negres Marine Reserve, off the coast of Spain's Catalonia region. Its underwater treasures include coral reefs and sea-grass meadows, which are habitats for sea snails, sea fans, and groupers. Site managers plan to install buoys to anchor boats above the sea-grass meadows in an ecological way, study a species of sea snail known as dog winkles, and reintroduce a type of sea snail that used to live there.

Another Natura 2000 site is Estonia's Kihnu Strait Marine Park. Its protected species include seals, toads, and waterbirds such as swans, terns, geese, crakes, and ruffs. Among the site's management goals is to decrease the negative impacts of seal hunting, wildfowl egg gathering, and other traditional activities. As in all Natura 2000 sites, the local community is involved in helping to support and maintain the site, gather useful information, and promote ecological goals.

Community-Based Strategies

You do not have to be a Coast Guard officer, fish and wildlife inspector, environmental engineer, marine researcher, industrial leader, or government policy maker to be involved in ocean management. In fact, these people cannot do an effective job without ordinary citizens doing their part from the ground up. Here are some ways that you and others in your community can help combat ocean pollution and preserve marine ecosystems.

- Beaches, shores, and boating areas are great recreation spots. While you are there, pick up all garbage, litter, and equipment before you go. Leave the area cleaner than you found it.

You can help with the preservation of the ocean by cleaning litter from local marine areas through volunteer programs.

- Recycle as much of your garbage as possible to reduce the amount of debris in landfills. Runoff from the landfill carries pollutants overland and underground into the waterways.

- Cut the rings of plastic six-pack holders. Turtles, birds, and other creatures can get tangled in them.

- Minimize your pollution footprint. Pollutants you use every day can end up in the oceans via runoff or in airborne form. Dispose of paint, cleaning fluids, batteries, and motor oil properly. Avoid using chemical insecticides, and use clippings or compost instead of chemical fertilizers. Use phosphate-free detergents. Drive a fuel-efficient car, or use an alternative-fuel vehicle; keep cars in good repair so that they do not leak oil. Ride a bike or walk instead of driving. Reduce your use of plastic products by using reusable water bottles and grocery bags and buying products with minimal plastic packaging.

- Notify local environmental agencies if you encounter wastes discharged directly into a waterway.

- Notify local environmental agencies if you encounter coastal areas that are polluted, contaminated, littered, or strewn with injured, sick, or dead wildlife.

- If you live near an ocean, river, or lake, organize a community cleanup project alongside it.

- Visit a water-treatment plant or water-testing lab to see how scientists eliminate pollutants and test for water quality.

- As volunteer or a student intern, take part in a water-quality survey or marine research project.

- Be aware of development projects in your region that could impact water quality. Information is available through online notices, TV and radio newscasts, local and national newspaper articles, public exhibits and displays, and leaflets, brochures, and newsletters.

- Gather information. Study the issues, and read experts' assessments of the project's environmental impact. Attend public hearings, citizens' action meetings, press conferences, or other community information forums.

- Get involved. If you feel strongly about a proposed project's environmental impact, contribute to online discussion forums, call staffed phone lines with comments, take part in letter-writing campaigns, or help with collecting signatures on petitions.

- Let your U.S. senators and representatives know that you favor clean-water legislation, antidumping measures, and stricter regulations for industrial waste disposal.

Vast and complex, the oceans provide us with oxygen, a livable climate, food, transportation, recreation, and jobs. It is in the best interests of the world community to keep our ocean waters clean and safe and our marine ecosystems healthy.

The power and beauty of the world's oceans can be maintained through shared responsibility among us all.

As we have discovered, the oceans are sensitive to human interference because of the intricate interrelationships between the physical ocean, marine life, and human activities. In taking the oceans for granted as a limitless resource, we are abusing them. Unbridled industrialization threatens the oceans' dynamic processes that stabilize the planet. Unrestrained exploitation jeopardizes the biodiversity that makes the ocean a vibrant ecosystem and a productive source of food.

Clearly, we must restore and maintain the oceans' vitality. Yet we face many challenges in doing so. There is a constant tension between immediate economic imperatives and a long-range vision of sustainability. Only through shared responsibility in ocean management—from the global sphere on down to the local level—can we protect the oceans' priceless resources for future generations.

Notes

Chapter One

p. 7, "[T]he sea is common to all, . . . ": Hugo Grotius, The Freedom of the Sea (trans. of Mare Liberum by Ralph Van Deman Magoffin), New York: Oxford University Press, 1916, Online Library of Liberty, p. 64, http://oll. libertyfund.org/title/552 (accessed May 24, 2010).

p. 7, "Oceans . . . Earth's water.": "Ocean," National Oceanic and Atmospheric Administration (NOAA), www.noaa. gov/ocean.html (accessed May 13, 2010).

p. 7, "They support . . . humans consume.": "Ocean," National Oceanic and Atmospheric Administration (NOAA).

p. 8, "Economists estimate . . . domestic product.": "Ocean," National Oceanic and Atmospheric Administration (NOAA).

p. 8, " . . . almost quadrupled . . . ": "Water and Population," ch. 2 of The State of World Population 2001, Environmental Trends, UN Population Fund (UNFPA), www.unfpa.org/ swp/2001/english/ch02.html (accessed May 24, 2010).

p. 9, "... 3 nautical miles ... from shore.": Robert Jay Wilder, *Listening to the Sea: The Politics of Improving Environmental Protection* (Pittsburgh: University of Pittsburgh Press, 1998), p. 14.

p. 9, "In a 2008 ... human factors.": Benjamin S. Halpern et al., "A Global Map of Human Impact on Marine Ecosystems," *Science*, February 15, 2008, www.sciencemag.org/cgi/content/full/319/5865/948 (accessed August 3, 2010).

Chapter Two

p. 15, "Amazingly, ... humans breathe.": "Carbon Cycle," NASA Science, http://science.nasa.gov/earth-science/oceanography/ocean-earth-system/ocean-carbon-cycle/ (accessed May 13, 2010).

p. 16, "Carbon sinks have ... combined.": "Vital Ocean 'Carbon Sink' Nearly Full," Discovery Channel, May 17, 2007, http://dsc.discovery.com/news/2007/05/17/southernocean_pla.html?category = earth (accessed May 26, 2010).

p. 16, "The Southern Ocean, ... saturation point.": "Vital Ocean 'Carbon Sink' Nearly Full," Discovery Channel.

p. 20, "Canada's Bay ... twice a day.": "Bay of Fundy: The Highest Tides in the World," NOAA, National Weather Service, www.srh.noaa.gov/jetstream/ocean/fundy_max.htm (accessed May 18, 2010).

p. 22, "The surface layer ... the polar seas.": "Temperature of Ocean Water," *Windows to the Universe*, National Earth Science Teachers Association (NESTA), www.windows2universe.org/earth/Water/temp.html&edu = high (accessed May 18, 2010).

p. 22, " . . . ;much of the deep layer has . . . (−1.9 °C).": "Temperature of Ocean Water," *Windows to the Universe*, National Earth Science Teachers Association (NESTA).

p. 23, "Scientists use . . . oceanic zone.": "Zonation and Distribution, Part I," USC Sea Grant Island Explorers, www.usc.edu/org/seagrant/Education/IELessons/Docs/ZonationDistributionPt1.pdf (accessed May 18, 2010).

Chapter Three

p. 30, "These so-called . . . in the United States.": Rob Magnien, "Diving Deeper: Dead Zone," NOAA podcast, July 1, 2009, http://oceanservice.noaa.gov/podcast/supp_july09.html#deadzone (accessed August 6, 2010).

p. 30, "According to . . . vessels.": *Ecosystems and Biodiversity in Deep Waters and High Seas*, UN Environment Programme, UNEP Regional Seas Reports and Studies, no. 178, UNEP/IUCN, Switzerland, 2006, p. 20, www.unep.org/pdf/EcosystemBiodiversity_DeepWaters_20060616.pdf (accessed December 28, 2009).

p. 32, "Ocean sailor . . . never flushes.": Jo Royle, "Antarctic trash led to mission to clean up the planet," CNN Tech, April 26, 2010, www.cnn.com/2010/TECH/04/26/opinion.joroyle.plastiki/index.html (accessed May 25, 2010).

p. 32, "Scientists estimate . . . on the surface.": Brian Handwerk, "Giant Ocean-Trash Vortex Attracts Explorers," *National Geographic News*, July 31, 2009, http://news.nationalgeographic.com/news/2009/07/090731-ocean-trash-pacific.html (accessed May 25, 2010).

p. 34, "When wildlife . . . this problem.": David Shukman, "New 'Battle of Midway' over Plastic," BBC News, March 26, 2008, http://news.bbc.co.uk/2/hi/science/nature/7314240.stm (accessed May 25, 2010).

p. 35, " . . . to dispose of . . . storage (CCS).": "EPA Proposes New Requirements for Geologic Sequestration of Carbon Dioxide," U.S. Environmental Protection Agency, EPA 816-F-08-032, July 2008, www.epa.gov/ogwdw000/uic/pdfs/fs_uic_co2_proposedrule.pdf (accessed August 6, 2010).

Chapter Four

p. 44, "Usually a consortium, . . . biodegradation.": "Oil Biodegradation: Bacterial Alteration of Petroleum," Oil Tracers LLC, 2010, www.oiltracers.com/services/exploration-geochemistry/oil-biodegradation.aspx (accessed August 4, 2010).

p. 44, "Some oil components . . . process the oil.": "Oil Biodegradation: Bacterial Alteration of Petroleum," Oil Tracers LLC.

p. 45, "When fish are exposed . . . as well as usual.": "Oil spills can be very harmful to marine birds and mammals as well as fish and shellfish," NOAA, National Ocean Service, http://oceanservice.noaa.gov/facts/oilimpacts.html (accessed May 20, 2010).

p. 45, "For most . . . inland waters.": "Natural Resource Damages: A Primer," U.S. Environmental Protection Agency, www.epa.gov/superfund/programs/nrd/primer.htm (accessed May 25, 2010).

p. 47, "Also, in testing . . . crude oil.": "Oil Spill Clean-Up Agents Threaten Coral Reefs," *ScienceDaily*, July 31, 2007, www.sciencedaily.com/releases/2007/07/070730172426.htm (accessed May 25, 2010).

p. 47, " . . . about 11 million . . . destroyed, too.": "Oil Spill Facts: Questions and Answers," Exxon Valdez Oil Spill Trustee Council, www.evostc.state.ak.us/facts/qanda.cfm (accessed May 31, 2010).

p. 49, "They reported . . . continuing to decline.": *Exxon Valdez Oil Spill Restoration Plan: 2010 Update, Injured Resources and Services*, Exxon Valdez Oil Spill Trustee Council, May 14, 2010, www.evostc.state.ak.us/Universal/Documents/Publications/2010IRSUpdate.pdf, p. 7 (accessed May 31, 2010).

p. 50, Studies of . . . after the spill.": Daniel Esler et al., "Cytochrome P4501A biomarker indication of oil exposure in harlequin ducks up to 20 years after the *Exxon Valdez* oil spill," *Environmental Toxicology and Chemistry* 29, no. 5, January 21, 2010, pp. 1138–1145, www3.interscience. wiley.com/journal/123250065/abstract?CRETRY = 1&SRETRY = 0 (accessed May 31, 2010).

p. 50, "In 2007, . . . significant.": Elizabeth Weise, "Damage of Exxon Valdez endures," *USA Today*, February 1, 2007, www.usatoday.com/news/nation/2007-01-31-exxon-alaska_x.htm (accessed May 31, 2010).

p. 50, "According to NOAA . . . percent a year.": Weise, "Damage of Exxon Valdez endures," *USA Today*.

Chapter Five

p. 51, "In fact, . . . animal protein.": *The State of World Fisheries and Aquaculture, 2000*, FAO Fisheries and Agriculture Department (Rome: Food and Agriculture Organization, 2001), www.fao.org/docrep/003/x8002e/x8002e04.htm (accessed May 27, 2010).

p. 51, "The worldwide . . . in 2003.": "World Marine Fish Catch: 80 Million Tons a Year," Progressive Policy Institute, August 23, 2006, www.ppionline.org/ppi_ci. cfm?knlgAreaID = 108&subsecID = 900003&contentI D = 254021 (accessed May 30, 2010).

p. 53, "According to . . . collapsed.": Camilo Mora et al.,

"Management Effectiveness of the World's Marine Fisheries," *PLoS Biology* 7(6): e1000131, June 23, 2009, www.plosbiology.org/article/info%3Adoi%2F10.1371%2 Fjournal.pbio.1000131 (accessed May 27, 2010).

p. 53, "The only seafood . . . flounder).": "Tuna: Protecting the most commercially valuable fish on the planet," World Wildlife Fund, www.worldwildlife.org/species/finder/ tuna/index.html (accessed April 9, 2010).

p. 53, "Researchers estimate . . . a year.": *Ecosystems and Biodiversity*, UNEP, p. 52.

p. 54, "For every pound . . . every year.": "Red Fish Fact Sheets: Tropical Shrimp," Greenpeace USA, www.greenpeace. org/usa/campaigns/oceans/seafood/red-fish (accessed April 9, 2010).

p. 54, "According to . . . food chain.": "Waste Disposal and Reduction," UN System-Wide Earthwatch, http:// earthwatch.unep.net/emergingissues/solidwaste/ wastedisposal.php (accessed May 27, 2010).

p. 55, "Tuna generally . . . light tuna.": "What You Need to Know about Mercury in Fish and Shellfish," U.S. Environmental Protection Agency (EPA), www.epa.gov/ waterscience/fish/advice/ (accessed May 27, 2010).

p. 55, "A study . . . saturated fats.": C. F. van Kreijl et al. (eds.), *Our Food, Our Health: Healthy Diet and Safe Food in the Netherlands*, Bilthoven, The Netherlands: National Institute for Public Health and the Environment, 2006, p. 33, www.rivm.nl/bibliotheek/rapporten/270555009. pdf (accessed August 5, 2010).

p. 56, "In the European . . . entire production.": "Aquaculture: Fish Farming," European Fisheries Commission, http:// ec.europa.eu/fisheries/cfp/aquaculture/index_en.htm (accessed August 9, 2010).

p. 56, "About half . . . from fish farms.": "Aquaculture," Monterey Bay Aquarium, www.montereybayaquarium. org/cr/cr_seafoodwatch/issues/aquaculture.aspx (accessed August 9, 2010).

p. 56, "According to the UN's . . . food fish.": "Aquaculture," Fisheries and Aquaculture Department, Food and Agriculture Organization of the United Nations, www.fao. org/fishery/aquaculture/en (accessed August 9, 2010).

p. 56, "About half . . . marine species.": *State of World Aquaculture 2006*, Rome: Food and Agriculture Organization, 2006, p. 10, www.fao.org/docrep/009/a0874e/a0874e00. htm#Contents (accessed August 9, 2010).

p. 57, "A farmed salmon, . . . pound of weight.": "Agriculture Issue: Use of Wild Fish," Monterey Bay Aquarium, www. montereybayaquarium.org/cr/cr_seafoodwatch/issues/ aquaculture_wildfish.aspx (accessed August 9, 2010).

p. 57, "Aquaculturists in Norway . . . banned altogether.": *State of World Aquaculture 2006*, p. 63.

p. 58, "Some countries . . . bycatch restrictions.": Mora et al., "Management Effectiveness."

p. 59, "As of 2006, . . . antifreeze.": *Ecosystems and Biodiversity*, UNEP, p. 21.

p. 61, "One Scottish fisherman . . . 'euro-conservation'.": "Common Fisheries Policy," Civitas: EU Facts, May 8, 2010, www.civitas.org.uk/eufacts/FSPOL/AG5.htm (accessed August 9, 2010).

p. 61, "Scotland's World . . . jobs for communities.": "Fish Policy Blighted by 'Failure,'" BBC News, September 20, 2009, http://news.bbc.co.uk/2/hi/uk_news/scotland/ north_east/8263219.stm (accessed August 9, 2010).

p. 61, "Realizing . . . own fisheries.": European Fisheries Commission, Synthesis of the Consultation on the Reform of the Common Fisheries Policy, Commission Staff Working Document, Brussels, Belgium, April 16, 2010, http://ec.europa.eu/fisheries/reform/sec(2010)0428_ en.pdf (accessed August 9, 2010).

Chapter Six

p. 63, "When people share . . . 'coercive laws.'": Garrett Hardin, "The Tragedy of the Commons," *Science*, December 13, 1968, also in The Garrett Hardin Society, www. garretthardinsociety.org/articles/art_tragedy_of_the_ commons.html (accessed May 29, 2010).

p. 65, "As of October . . . international shipping.": International Maritime Organization, www.imo.org/conventions/ asp?topic_id = 247 (accessed October 21, 2010).

p. 67, "Drifting particles . . . rain clouds.": Jean-Marc Brignon and Guy Landrieu, "Integrating the Environmental Effects of Particulate Matter in Emission Control Strategies," Task Force on Integrated Assessment Modelling, 26th session, Brussels, May 14–16, 2001, www.unece. org/env/lrtap/TaskForce/tfiam/26meeting/ineris_ tfiam26.doc (accessed May 22, 2010).

p. 69, "Under the MMPA, . . . these animals.": Jason Parent, "The MMPA, U.S. Endangered Species Protection: Marine Mammal Protection Act Protects Whales, Dolphins, and Seals," *Suite 101: Wildlife Preservation*, http://wildlifepreservation.suite101.com/article. cfm/the_mmpa_us_endangered_species_protection (accessed May 22, 2010).

Chapter Seven

p. 74, "More than seventy . . . transparent processes.": Neil Craik, *The International Law of Environmental*

Impact Assessment: Process, Substance and Integration (Cambridge, UK: Cambridge University Press, 2008), pp. 42–44.

p. 77, "The London Protocol has approved . . . formations.": London Protocol: Specific Guidelines for Assessment of Carbon Dioxide Streams for Disposal into Subseabed Geological Formations, International Maritime Organization, www.imo.org/includes/blastData.asp/doc_id = 10531/9 % 20- % 20CO2 % 20Sequestration % 20 English.pdf (accessed May 20, 2010).

p. 77, "Nevertheless, . . . 1996.": Robin Warner, *Climate Change Mitigation Activities in the Oceans: Regulatory Frameworks and Implications*, Australian National Centre for Ocean Resources and Security, p. 14, www. iwlearn.net/abt_iwlearn/events/.../warner_iwc5_ mitigation.pdf (accessed May 21, 2010).

Further Information

Books

Aleshire, Peter. *Ocean Ridges and Trenches*. New York: Chelsea House, 2007.

Day, Trevor, and Richard Garratt, illus. *Oceans* (Ecosystem). New York: Facts on File, 2007.

Foran, Jill. *A Planet Choking on Waste* (Understanding Global Issues). Calgary, AB: Weigl, 2008.

Kaye, Cathryn Berger, and Philippe Cousteau. *Going Blue: A Teen Guide to Saving Our Oceans, Lakes, Rivers and Wetlands*. Minneapolis: Free Spirit, 2010.

Kusky, Timothy. *The Coast: Hazardous Interactions within the Coastal Environment*. New York: Facts on File, 2008.

Leacock, Elspeth. *The Exxon Valdez Oil Spill* (Environmental Disasters). New York: Facts on File, 2005.

Petersen, Christine. *Renewing Earth's Waters* (Environment at Risk). New York: Marshall Cavendish Benchmark, 2011.

Sawvel, Patty Jo. *Water Resource Management*. Detroit: Gale/ Cengage Learning, 2008.

Websites
Biodiversity and Climate Change 2000: Changing Oceans
www.unep-wcmc.org/climate/oceans/intro.aspx
The UN Environment Programme's studies on climate and ocean ecosystems.

Earth's Ocean (National Earth Science Teachers Association)
www.windows2universe.org/earth/Water/ocean.
html&edu = high
Broad coverage of the oceans from an earth science perspective.

International Maritime Organization
www.imo.org/
Includes information on the marine environment, human impact on the oceans, and international agreements on marine pollution.

NASA Oceanography
http://science.nasa.gov/earth-science/oceanography/
Covers the oceans' physical properties, organisms, and role in Earth's climate.

Ocean Facts (National Oceanic and Atmospheric Administration)
http://oceanservice.noaa.gov/facts/welcome.html
Extensive information on ocean life, geology, and management.

Oceans, Coasts, and Estuaries (Environmental Protection Agency)
www.epa.gov/owow/oceans/
An environmental perspective on ocean protection and coastal management.

Seafood Watch

www.montereybayaquarium.org/cr/cr_seafoodwatch/sfw_
recommendations.aspx

The Monterey Bay (California) Aquarium's guide to
recommended seafoods for consumption; takes into account
both contaminants and fishing methods.

Bibliography

Books and Pamphlets
Craik, Neil. *The International Law of Environmental Impact Assessment: Process, Substance and Integration.* Cambridge, UK: Cambridge University Press, 2008.

European Commission: Fisheries. *The Ecosystem Approach to Fisheries: Fact Sheet.* http://ec.europa.eu/fisheries/documentation/publications/cfp_factsheets/ecosystem_approach_en.pdf (accessed August 7, 2010). N.d.

———. Synthesis of the Consultation on the Reform of the Common Fisheries Policy. Commission Staff Working Document. Brussels: April 16, 2010. http://ec.europa.eu/fisheries/reform/sec(2010)0428_en.pdf (accessed August 9, 2010).

Exxon Valdez Oil Spill Trustee Council. *Exxon Valdez Oil Spill Restoration Plan: 2010 Update, Injured Resources and Services.* May 14, 2010. www.evostc.state.ak.us/Universal/Documents/Publications/2010IRSUpdate.pdf (accessed May 31, 2010).

Food and Agriculture Organization of the United Nations (FAO). Fisheries and Aquaculture Department. *State of World Aquaculture 2006.* Rome: Food and Agriculture Organization, 2006. www.fao.org/docrep/009/a0874e/a0874e00.htm#Contents (accessed August 9, 2010).

Frankel, Ernst G. *Ocean Environmental Management: A Primer on the Role of the Oceans and How to Maintain Their Contributions to Life on Earth.* Englewood Cliffs, NJ: Prentice Hall, 1995.

Glasson, John, Riki Therivel, and Andrew Chadwick. *Introduction to Environmental Impact Assessment.* New York: Routledge, 2005.

Grotius, Hugo. *The Freedom of the Sea.* Trans. of *Mare Liberum* by Ralph Van Deman Magoffin. New York: Oxford University Press, 1916. Online Library of Liberty, http://oll.libertyfund.org/title/552, p. 64 (accessed May 24, 2010).

Tay, Kok-Leng, James Osborne, and Lawrence K. Wang. "Ocean Disposal Technology and Assessment." Ch. 9 of Lawrence K. Wang et al., *Biosolids Engineering and Management,* vol. 7. Totowa, NJ: Humana Press, 2008.

United Nations. *Oceans: The Source of Life.* UN Convention on the Law of the Sea: 20th Anniversary (1982–2002). www.un.org/depts/los/convention_agreements/convention_20years/oceanssourceoflife.pdf (accessed May 22, 2010).

United Nations Environment Programme (UNEP). *Ecosystems and Biodiversity in Deep Waters and High Seas.* UNEP Regional Seas Reports and Studies, no. 178. UNEP/IUCN, Switzerland, 2006. www.unep.org/pdf/EcosystemBiodiversity_DeepWaters_20060616.pdf (accessed Dec-ember 28, 2009).

Warner, Robin. *Climate Change Mitigation Activities in the Oceans: Regulatory Frameworks and Implications.* Australian National Centre for Ocean Resources and Security. www.iwlearn.net/abt_iwlearn/events/iwc5/iwc5_presentations/warner_iwc5_mitigation.pdf (accessed May 21, 2010).

Wilder, Robert Jay. *Listening to the Sea: The Politics of Improving Environmental Protection.* Pittsburgh: University of Pittsburgh Press, 1998.

World Health Organization (WHO). *Guidelines for Drinking-Water Quality*, 3rd edition. Geneva: WHO, 2008. www.who.int/entity/water_sanitation_health/dwq/GDWAN4rev1and2.pdf (accessed August 5, 2010).

Journal Articles and Conference Papers

Brignon, Jean-Marc, and Guy Landrieu. "Integrating the Environmental Effects of Particulate Matter in Emission Control Strategies." UNECE Task Force on Integrated Assessment Modelling, 26th session, Brussels, May 14–16, 2001. www.unece.org/env/lrtap/TaskForce/tfiam/26meeting/ineris_tfiam26.doc (accessed May 22, 2010).

Esler, Daniel, et al. "Cytochrome P4501: A Biomarker Indication of Oil Exposure in Harlequin Ducks up to 20 Years after the *Exxon Valdez* Oil Spill." *Environmental Toxicology and Chemistry* 29, no. 5 (January 21, 2010): 1138–1145. www3.interscience.wiley.com/journal/123250065/abstract?CRETRY = 1&SRETRY = 0 (accessed May 31, 2010).

Halpern, Benjamin S., et al. "A Global Map of Human Impact on Marine Ecosystems." *Science*, February 15, 2008. www.sciencemag.org/cgi/content/full/319/5865/948 (accessed August 3, 2010).

Hardin, Garrett. "The Tragedy of the Commons." *Science*, December 13, 1968. Also in The Garrett Hardin Society, www.garretthardinsociety.org/articles/art_tragedy_of_the_commons.html (accessed May 29, 2010).

Horstman, Erik M., et al. "On the consequences of a long-term perspective for coastal management." *Ocean & Coastal Management* 52, no. 12 (December 2009): 593–611.

Mora, Camilo, et al. "Management Effectiveness of the World's Marine Fisheries." *PLoS Biology* 7, no. 6: e1000131 (June 23, 2009). www.plosbiology.org/article/info % 3Adoi % 2F10.1371 % 2Fjournal.pbio.1000131 (accessed May 27, 2010).

99

Rochette, Julien, and Raphaël Billé. "Governance of Marine Biodiversity beyond National Jurisdictions: Issues and Perspectives." Report of the International Seminar "Towards a New Governance of High Seas Biodiversity," Principality of Monaco, March 20–21, 2008. *Ocean & Coastal Management* 51, no. 12 (December 2008): 779–781.

Worm, Boris, et al. "Impacts of Biodiversity Loss on Ocean Ecosystem Services." *Science* 314, no. 5800 (November 3, 2006): 787–790.

Websites
Civitas: EU Facts. "Common Fisheries Policy." May 8, 2010. www.civitas.org.uk/eufacts/FSPOL/AG5.htm (accessed August 9, 2010).

Discovery Channel. "Vital Ocean 'Carbon Sink' Nearly Full." May 17, 2007. http://dsc.discovery.com/news/2007/05/17/southernocean_pla.html?category = earth (accessed May 26, 2010).

Environmental Protection Agency (EPA). "Drinking Water Contaminants." www.epa.gov/safewater/contaminants/index.html (accessed August 5, 2010).

———. "EPA Proposes New Requirements for Geologic Sequestration of Carbon Dioxide." EPA 816-F-08-032, July 2008. www.epa.gov/ogwdw000/uic/pdfs/fs_uic_co2_proposedrule.pdf (accessed August 6, 2010).

———. "Natural Resource Damages: A Primer." www.epa.gov/superfund/programs/nrd/primer.htm (accessed May 25, 2010).

———. "What You Need to Know about Mercury in Fish and Shellfish." www.epa.gov/waterscience/fish/advice/ (accessed May 27, 2010).

European Commission: Fisheries. "Aquaculture: Fish Farming." http://ec.europa.eu/fisheries/cfp/aquaculture/index_en.htm (accessed August 9, 2010).

———. "The Common Fisheries Policy (CFP)." http://ec.europa.eu/fisheries/cfp/index_en.htm (accessed August 7, 2010).

Exxon Valdez Oil Spill Trustee Council. "Oil Spill Facts: Questions and Answers." www.evostc.state.ak.us/facts/qanda.cfm (accessed May 31, 2010).

Food and Agriculture Organization of the United Nations (FAO). Fisheries and Aquaculture Department. "Aquaculture." www.fao.org/fishery/aquaculture/en (accessed August 9, 2010).

———. "Fishing Gears and Methods." http://www.fao.org/fishery/topic/1617/en (accessed April 9, 2010).

———. The State of World Fisheries and Aquaculture, 2000. Rome: Food and Agriculture Organization, 2001. www.fao.org/docrep/003/x8002e/x8002e04.htm (accessed May 27, 2010).

Greenpeace USA. "Red Fish Fact Sheets." www.greenpeace.org/usa/campaigns/oceans/seafood/red-fish (accessed April 9, 2010).

Handwerk, Brian. "Giant Ocean-Trash Vortex Attracts Explorers." National Geographic News, July 31, 2009, http://news.nationalgeographic.com/news/2009/07/090731-ocean-trash-pacific.html (accessed May 25, 2010).

International Maritime Organization. International Convention for the Prevention of Pollution from Ships, 1973, as modified by the Protocol of 1978 relating thereto (MARPOL). www.imo.org/conventions/contents.asp?doc_id = 678& topic_id = 258 (accessed March 15, 2010).

———. International Convention on Oil Pollution Preparedness, Response and Co-operation, 1990. www.imo.org/

conventions/mainframe.asp?topic_id = 258&doc_id = 682 (accessed May 14, 2010).

———. London Convention and Protocol: Convention on the Prevention of Marine Pollution by Dumping of Wastes and Other Matter 1972 and 1996 Protocol Thereto. www.imo.org/home.asp?topic_id = 1488 (accessed May 20, 2010).

———. The London Convention and Protocol: Their Role and Contribution to Protection of the Marine Environment. www.imo.org/includes/blastData.asp?doc_id = 7487&type = body (accessed May 20, 2010).

———. London Protocol: Specific Guidelines for Assessment of Carbon Dioxide Streams for Disposal into Sub-seabed Geological Formations. www.imo.org/includes/blastData.asp/doc_id = 10531/9 % 20- % 20CO2 % 20Sequestration % 20 English.pdf (accessed May 20, 2010).

International Union for Conservation of Nature. "The IUCN Red List of Threatened Species," version 2010.1. IUCN 2010. www.iucnredlist.org/ (accessed April 9, 2010).

National Aeronautics and Space Administration. "Carbon Cycle." NASA Science. http://science.nasa.gov/earth-science/oceanography/ocean-earth-system/ocean-carbon-cycle/ (accessed May 13, 2010).

National Earth Science Teachers Association (NESTA). "Temperature of Ocean Water." Windows to the Universe. www.windows2universe.org/earth/Water/temp.html&edu = high (accessed May 18, 2010).

National Oceanic and Atmospheric Administration (NOAA). "Bay of Fundy: The Highest Tides in the World." National Weather Service. www.srh.noaa.gov/jetstream/ocean/fundy_max.htm (accessed May 18, 2010).

———. "Diving Deeper: Dead Zone." Podcast interview with

Rob Magnien, July 1, 2009. http://oceanservice.noaa.gov/podcast/supp_july09.html#deadzone (accessed August 6, 2010).

———. "Information on Marine Debris." National Ocean Service, Office of Response and Restoration. http://marinedebris.noaa.gov/info/welcome.html (accessed May 25, 2010).

———. "Ocean." www.noaa.gov/ocean.html (accessed May 13, 2010).

———. "Oil spills can be very harmful to marine birds and mammals as well as fish and shellfish." National Ocean Service. http://oceanservice.noaa.gov/facts/oilimpacts.html (accessed May 20, 2010).

OCS [Outer Continental Shelf] Alternative Energy and Alternate Use Programmatic EIS Information Center. *Alternative Energy and Alternate Use Guide.* http://ocsenergy.anl.gov/guide/index.cfm (accessed May 20, 2010).

Parent, Jason. "The MMPA, U.S. Endangered Species Protection: Marine Mammal Protection Act Protects Whales, Dolphins, and Seals." *Suite 101: Wildlife Preservation.* http://wildlifepreservation.suite101.com/article.cfm/the_mmpa_us_endangered_species_protection (accessed May 22, 2010).

Progressive Policy Institute. "World Marine Fish Catch: 80 Million Tons a Year." August 23, 2006. www.ppionline.org/ppi_ci.cfm?knlgAreaID = 108&subsecID = 900003&contentID = 254021 (accessed May 30, 2010).

Restore the Gulf. Deepwater Horizon Unified Command. www.restorethegulf.gov/ (accessed August 6, 2010).

Royle, Jo. "Antarctic trash led to mission to clean up the planet." CNN Tech, April 26, 2010. www.cnn.com/2010/TECH/04/26/opinion.joroyle.plastiki/index.html (accessed May 25, 2010).

ScienceDaily. "Oil Spill Clean-Up Agents Threaten Coral

Reefs." July 31, 2007. www.sciencedaily.com/releases/2007/07/070730172426.htm (accessed May 25, 2010).

Shukman, David. "New 'Battle of Midway' over Plastic." BBC News, March 26, 2008. http://news.bbc.co.uk/2/hi/science/nature/7314240.stm (accessed May 25, 2010).

University of Southern California. "Zonation and Distribution, Part I." USC Sea Grant Island Explorers. www.usc.edu/org/seagrant/Education/IELessons/Docs/ZonationDistribution Pt1.pdf (accessed May 18, 2010).

UN Atlas of the Oceans. "About the Oceans." www.oceansatlas. org/html/workabout.jsp (accessed December 28, 2009).

UN Environment Programme (UNEP). "The Global "Programme of Action for the Protection of the Marine Environment from Land-Based Activities." www.gpa.unep. org/ (accessed May 22, 2010).

UN Population Fund (UNFPA). "Water and Population." In *The State of World Population 2001*, chap. 2, "Environmental Trends." www.unfpa.org/swp/2001/english/ch02.html (accessed May 24, 2010).

UN System-Wide Earthwatch. "Waste Disposal and Reduction." http://earthwatch.unep.net/emergingissues/solidwaste/wastedisposal.php (accessed May 27, 2010).

Van Kreijl, C. F., et al., eds. *Our Food, Our Health: Healthy Diet and Safe Food in the Netherlands*. Bilthoven, The Netherlands: National Institute for Public Health and the Environment, 2006. www.rivm.nl/bibliotheek/rapporten/270555009.pdf (accessed August 5, 2010).

Weise, Elizabeth. "Damage of Exxon Valdez Endures." *USA Today*, February 1, 2007. www.usatoday.com/news/nation/2007-01-31-exxon-alaska_x.htm (accessed May 31, 2010).

World Wildlife Fund. "Tuna: Protecting the Most Commercially Valuable Fish on the Planet." www.worldwildlife.org/species/ finder/tuna/index.html (accessed April 9, 2010).

Index

Page numbers in **boldface** are illustrations.

About the Author

Ann Heinrichs is the award-winning author of more than two hundred books on U.S. and world history, geography, culture, and political affairs. She has also written on topics in the fields of science and nature, biography, and English grammar and formerly worked as a children's book editor and an advertising copywriter. World exploration is her passion; she has traveled through Africa, the Middle East, Europe, and East Asia. After many crossings, her favorite sea is the South China Sea, an arm of the western Pacific Ocean. Heinrichs lives in Chicago, Illinois, where she enjoys bicycling and kayaking.